The Capitol
Seventh Edition

Contents

95th Congress, 1st Session,
H. Con. Res. 222, House Document No. 95–260

W9-CTR-661

The Statue of Freedom atop the Capitol dome. Sculptured in Italy by the American, Thomas Crawford, for $3,000, and installed in 1863, it is 19 feet 6 inches tall and weighs 14,985 pounds. Total cost $23,796.82. It was placed in position amid a proud salute of 35 guns (one for each State) on December 2, 1863, during Lincoln's first term.

Foreword

The purpose of this publication is to provide a pictorial history of the Capitol and the Congress. **The Capitol** publication was initiated in the Eighty-fourth Congress with the support of the late Speaker Sam Rayburn. This seventh edition focuses not only on the Capitol as an historical edifice, but on the Congress as a living and dynamic institution within our Federal Government.

The Capitol of the United States is a landmark well known to the American people. Presidents are inaugurated in front of it; Congressmen pose beside it; tourists swarm over it; and artists study it. Within its walls the first branch of Government—the Congress of the United States—deliberates, debates and decides policies which govern the Nation.

Construction of the building began in 1793 when President George Washington laid the cornerstone on Jenkins Hill — described by Major Pierre Charles L'Enfant, the architect of Washington, D.C., as "a pedestal waiting for a monument". The Capitol was built in five major sections, the first of which was the north wing occupied by Congress and the Supreme Court when the government moved to Washington from Philadelphia in 1800.

The Capitol not only serves as the seat of our legislature, but is also a museum filled with artistic treasures. Its collection includes portraits and statues of past political leaders and of others who have influenced the history of our country. Statuary Hall, located in what originally was the House Chamber, contains statues from every state in the Union in order to remind us of our forefathers and their contribution to our growth as a Nation.

This seventh edition of **The Capitol** has been compiled under the direction of the Joint Committee on Printing, which has the responsibility and jurisdiction for the printing and distribution of Government documents. In the Ninety-first Congress the Joint Committee began alternating its chairmanship between its House and Senate Members. Representative Frank Thompson, Jr. of New Jersey is serving as chairman during the Ninety-sixth Congress.

The successful compilation of any publication includes the efforts and talents of many individuals. In that context, Chairman Frank Thompson, Jr. and Vice Chairman Claiborne Pell and the Members of the Joint Committee on Printing wish to recognize and express their appreciation for the dedication and cooperative teamwork of the staffs of the Committee on House Administration and the Senate Committee on Rules and Administration.

Our thanks also go to those in the office of the Architect of the Capitol, the Superintendent of Typography and Design at the Government Printing Office, and the Congressional Research Service in the Library of Congress, all of whose assistance was notably helpful.

The Joint Committee on Printing

Chairman
Representative
Frank Thompson, Jr.
(D) New Jersey

Vice Chairman
Senator Claiborne Pell
(D) Rhode Island

Senator
Howard W. Cannon
(D) Nevada

Senator
Mark O. Hatfield
(R) Oregon

Representative
Augustus F. Hawkins
(D) California

Representative
William L. Dickinson
(R) Alabama

The Capitol—Its History and Architecture

Symbol of The Power of The People

The Capitol of the United States represents Government of the people, by the people, and for the people. The building shows the architectural direction and thinking of George Washington and Thomas Jefferson, both of whom were schooled in architecture.

5

Inception and Growth

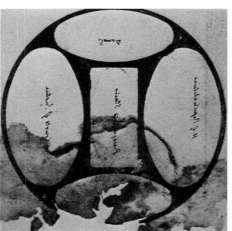

The announcement for the Capitol Competition of 1792 offered a lot in the city and $500 for the winning design.

The U.S. Capitol is the physical embodiment of the ideals and history of this country; the massive cast iron dome has become a symbol that has worldwide recognition. Millions visit the Capitol each year, and their memories are imprinted with the bustle of the House of Representatives and Senate, the incomparable view down the Mall from the West Front terraces, and the magnificence of the Rotunda, Statuary Hall and works of art. To those whose acquaintance with the Capitol is drawn from photographs in books, newspapers, and magazines, or from television and radio broadcasts, the great State occasions that take place in the building may seem most compelling. These Americans are more likely to remember ceremonies such as inaugurations, the Presidents' annual State of the Union messages, or the moments of national grief when our greatest citizens have lain in state in the Rotunda. The Capitol is an extraordinary repository of art and craftsmanship, the seat of Congress, and a living structure; it is one which has been designed, built, rebuilt and inhabited over the years by lively, colorful, and dedicated people.

At the time of its inception, the Capitol seemed to many people to be on overly ambitious project for the United States to undertake. In 1792 the Commissioners of the District of Columbia announced a competition to select a design for the building which would house Congress, the Library of Congress and the Supreme Court. A very satisfactory plan for the President's House by James Hoban, an Irish-born architect who had settled in America, had already been accepted. While the competition for the Capitol Building produced some interesting designs, it presented nothing that seemed appropriate to the building's complex function and symbolic purpose. America's few architects were mostly self-trained men whose experience was limited primarily to homes or small-scale public buildings, and neither President Washington nor Secretary of State Thomas Jefferson was satisfied with the various designs submitted by the July 15th deadline.

In November of the same year, William Thornton, a young multi-talented physician, wrote to the Commissioners of the Federal District, asking permission to submit a late entry. Thornton was an accomplished artist and amateur architect, and had also taken part in the earliest steamboat experiments in America. Since leaving Philadelphia

Thomas Jefferson oversaw both competitions for the construction of the Capitol and the White House. This sketch was probably done by Benjamin Latrobe, the Second Architect of the Capitol, about 1799.

Although Thomas Jefferson did not enter the competition for the Capitol he did draw this theoretical plan. A student of antiquity, he used the perfect form, the circle, as the basis for his study.

in 1790, he had been living in his native Virgin Islands. Thornton's request was granted, and he returned at once to Philadelphia, submitting his design to President Washington in January, 1793. Washington was immediately impressed with the design, and soon wrote praising the plan for its "grandeur, simplicity, and beauty of the exterior". Thomas Jefferson eagerly concurred, writing that "Dr. Thornton's plan has . . . so captivated the eyes and judgment of all as to leave no doubt you will prefer it when it shall be exhibited to you". The finished version of his design delighted everyone except the runner-up, Stephen Hallet, a French-born architect who had seemed assured of winning the competition before Thornton's entry was submitted. As compensation, Hallet was awarded a $500 prize, the same as that granted Dr. Thornton, and he was placed in charge of actual construction of the

Capitol, thus initiating one of the many personality conflicts that attended the planning and design of the buildings of the new Capitol.

As early as 1783, the Continental Congress had resolved to establish two capital cities, one of which was to be located on the Potomac near Georgetown. The idea of a second city, which would have been located on the Delaware River above Trenton, New Jersey, had been discarded, and by January 1791 Major Pierre L'Enfant was appointed to design the new Federal City. Three months later George Washington issued a proclamation establishing the District of Columbia location.

Unfortunately, L'Enfant's temperament frequently placed him in conflict with his associates. One of these was Squire Daniel Carroll, an original landowner in the District of Columbia, who decided to build a new manor house on the site of one of the

Stephen Hallet was the runner-up for the Capitol Competition (1792). This elevation, though, shows the basic idea for the building's eventual construction. Thornton saw Hallet's work before making his own winning design.

This design for the East Front was drawn by Dr. Thornton and approved by George Washington. The wing on the right was completed first.

great avenues that L'Enfant planned to radiate in all directions from the Capitol. Unwilling to accept this intrusion on his grand design, L'Enfant sent a work crew to demolish the unfinished mansion which stood in the way of what would eventually become New Jersey Avenue. But Squire Carroll's uncle was also one of the three commissioners charged with the development of the city; combined with L'Enfant's other continuing disputes with the commissioners, this affair led to his dismissal by President Washington.

President Washington formally approved Dr. Thornton's revised design for the Capitol Building, and on September 18, 1793, he laid the Capitol's cornerstone in a Masonic ceremony in company with local officials. After the ceremony, in which the cornerstone was placed on a silver plate, an ox was roasted on a spit, and the assembled multitude ate and drank heartily until dusk. That event was both the first and last recorded occasion on which the cornerstone with its engraved silver plate was seen. In 1958, during the extension of the East Front, a determined but unsuccessful effort was made to find the stone.

Construction of the Capitol proceeded steadily after the festivities of the cornerstone-laying were over. Throughout this period a conflict was brewing between Dr. Thornton, who sought to preserve his design intact, and Stephen Hallet, the supervisor of construction, who began to introduce subtle changes in the design which were reminiscent of his own rejected plan. Thornton forced a confrontation,

On September 18, 1793, President George Washington laid the Capitol's cornerstone. This event was captured by artist Allyn Cox in the first floor corridor of the House Wing.

and the outraged Hallet was dismissed in 1794. The next superintendent of construction was George Hadfield, who arrived in 1795. Almost immediately he came under Dr. Thornton's criticism; Hadfield, though talented and dedicated, overstepped his authority, and he was dismissed three years later. In 1800, Congress was installed in the one completed wing of the Capitol.

In 1803 President Jefferson appointed Benjamin Latrobe, an academically-trained architect, to oversee the continuing construction of the Capitol. Since December, 1802, the House had been meeting in a temporary brick structure thrown up hastily on the foundations of its own wing. One story tall, oval and unbearably hot three seasons of the year, this structure was called "the Oven" by the Representatives who were unfortunate enough to meet in it. One of Latrobe's first acts was to order the demolition of "the Oven", and to raise the walls of the House wing. Work on it proceeded smoothly under Latrobe's guidance, but his prolific production of designs for other public and private buildings frequently directed his attention away from Washington, engendering considerable criticism. In response he appointed a fellow Englishman, John Lenthal, to be Clerk of the Works, with day-to-day responsibility for the Capitol when he himself was away. Lenthal took charge of the work with vigor, competence, and ability, but during one of Latrobe's extended absences in 1808, he removed the supports for the vaulting in the Supreme Court Chamber. The massive arches collapsed, killing Lenthal.

Upon the completion of the House wing, he substantially rebuilt the Senate wing which was plagued with leaks and falling plaster, although less than ten years old. His revised plan featured a handsome two-story Senate Chamber directly over the ground floor chamber of the Supreme Court. Both halls were recently restored as part of the Capitol's Bicentennial pro-

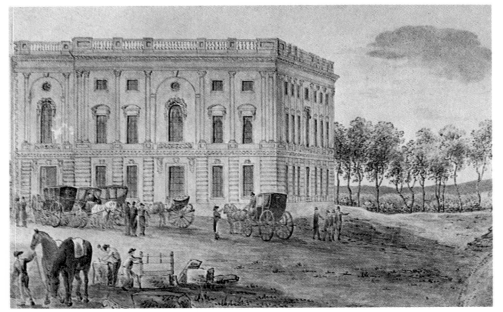

This is the Capitol when first occupied by Congress in 1800. The Supreme Court Chamber was on the first floor and the Senate Chamber occupied the second floor. Both Chambers have been restored.

gram, and are now open to visitors.

Under Latrobe's continued supervision, the House and Senate wings of the Capitol were virtually finished by 1811. Yet due to the imminence of war with Great Britain, the general appropriations for work on the Capitol ceased, and all plans for further improvement were put aside. In August of 1814, a British fleet appeared in the Chesapeake Bay with the determined purpose of capturing Washington; they brushed aside the opposing American militiamen at Bladensburg, and on the 24th of that month, marched into the Federal City. One of the British commanders, Rear Admiral Cockburn, led his men into the House Chamber, jumped up onto the Speaker's chair, and called the troops around him. Mocking legislative procedure, he asked the soldiers: "Shall this harbor of Yankee democracy be burned? All for it say 'aye'." The Admiral's motion passed unanimously, and the British troops set a great bonfire by piling desks, carpets, books, paintings, and everything else movable in the center of the Chamber, insuring a good blaze by sprinkling gunpowder over the pile before setting the torch to both wings. Late in the evening a violent thunderstorm drenched the burning buildings, saving them from total destruction.

Latrobe made several drawings that showed the extent of the damage, and then proceeded with reconstruction of the Capitol and the President's House; the exterior walls of both buildings were painted to hide the stains and scars left by the fires. Latrobe used that opportunity to alter Thornton's plan to his own tastes. He set to work with characteristic vigor, designing an enlarged Senate Chamber and a handsome semicircular room for the House of Representatives, which today is Statuary Hall. During the reconstruction, Congress met in a building where the Supreme Court now stands. This structure, the "Brick Capitol", was hastily erected in 1815 at the expense of some of Washington's businessmen, who feared that Congress would move the seat of Government away from the District of Columbia.

After Latrobe's resignation in 1817, Charles Bulfinch of Boston became

"Burning of the Capitol" depicted in mural by Allyn Cox, in the House corridor (1974).

This original drawing of the Capitol depicts the damage it sustained after it was burned by the British during the War of 1812.

Benjamin Latrobe proposed a Propylea type entrance for the West Front. Subsequently this part of the Capitol was altered and extended by Bulfinch.

This is the earliest known photograph of the Capitol. It is a daguerreotype and was probably taken by John Plumbe, Jr., reproduced in a lithographic print (called a Plumbeotype) and published around 1846. Water for non-culinary purposes was stored in the cistern seen in the center foreground.

The crypt with its 40 Doric columns supports the Rotunda which is directly above it. Built by Bulfinch, it is a showcase for its natural sandstone construction.

the third architect to shape the Capitol. Widely respected for his designs, which included the State Houses for Massachusetts and Connecticut and a number of hospitals, Bulfinch also appears to have possessed the tact and political sensitivity his predecessors had lacked. He served as Architect from 1818 until the Capitol was completed in 1829, when the position of Architect of the Capitol was abolished. It was Bulfinch who completed the central section of the building, including the lower walls of the handsome Rotunda familiar to tourists today. Although most of his work was done according to plans prepared by Latrobe, Bulfinch was able to put his personal stamp on the building in his execution of the extended West Front and the dome. Much criticism had been directed at the low height of the Rotunda dome as originally planned, and Bulfinch prepared several drawings of alternate solutions to the problem, including one dome of considerably greater height merely as a point of comparison. Upon submission of these designs to the Cabinet, the taller dome was selected as the most attractive solution despite Bulfinch's personal distaste for the design. He was ordered to go ahead with construction of the higher dome, built of masonry and wood with copper sheathing.

During the reconstruction after the fire, Congress decided to assign watchmen to keep strangers from wandering throughout the Capitol and grounds at night. Three watchmen and

one sergeant were hired in 1825; they constituted the first police force in the Federal District outside Georgetown, and were the forerunners of today's U.S. Capitol Police. These early watchmen served also as guides in the Capitol. With the influx of visitors from the Centennial Exposition in Philadelphia in 1876, a separate guide force was recruited, thus beginning the present day guide service.

In 1824 the Marquis de Lafayette, hero of the Revolution, returned to America for his first visit in forty years. The great general was given a warm welcome everywhere he traveled in the country, but nowhere was it more spontaneous or heartfelt than in the Chamber of the House of Representatives, where he was received by the Members on December 9, 1824. Unprompted, they rose to their feet to honor him, and then, as though two hundred men were a single person, they doffed their hats. This was a remarkable tribute according to the customs of the day. Members of Congress usually removed their hats only in the presence of the President, a reigning monarch, clergymen, or, of course, when meeting a lady. The rules of the House no longer allow hats to be worn in the Chamber.

Benjamin Latrobe's design for the reconstructed Capitol had included an important innovation, the Capitol's first sanitary facilities. Originally the Congress was accommodated for nearly two decades with facilities outside the building; in the delicate lan-

guage of the time, they were known as "necessaries". Latrobe, with characteristic ingenuity, provided water closets in the courtyards and in the Capitol. Water was carried to the roof of the building from nearby cisterns and poured down the drains which emptied at the foot of Capitol Hill. Before Washington had a city water system a large circular cistern on the East Front was kept filled with water for non-culinary use.

Washington was a small town, with little in the way of entertainment other than the business of legislation and government. Consequently, viewing the Congress while in session was one of the most important and liveliest diversions of the day. Ladies of the city frequently spent their afternoons in the House and Senate visitors' galleries watching the parliamentary maneuvering and debates. The Senate, in particular, was considered worthy of attendance; Henry Clay, John C. Calhoun, and Daniel Webster, three of the greatest orators in our history, were all Members of the Senate in the decades before 1850. On the day a burning issue was to be debated, the galleries in the Senate would begin to fill early in the morning; when the time came for the debate to begin, the more gallant Members of the Senate would give up their desks to the belles who could not crowd their way into the galleries. On warm days, the poorly ventilated Chamber would heat up quickly, and fruit and beverages were sometimes passed on long poles to the sweltering spectators.

Sam Houston, the father of Texan independence and statehood, was a colorful Senator of this era. He would lounge at his desk with the casual air of a frontiersman, whittling delicate wooden hearts which he passed up to the loveliest ladies in the gallery. He disdained the black broadcloth tail coats favored by many of his colleagues in favor of a more flamboyant wardrobe. A visitor once noted that his costume included a panther-skin vest, a brightly striped serape slung over his shoulder, and a generous sombrero.

For nearly 50 years this is where the Representatives met. This painting by Samuel F. B. Morse shows a night session of the House in 1822. The thick hangings deadened unwanted echoes.

An oil painting by an unknown artist depicts the Capitol from Pennsylvania Avenue about 1827.

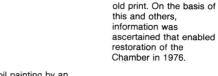

An 1842 session in the Senate is illustrated in this old print. On the basis of this and others, information was ascertained that enabled restoration of the Chamber in 1976.

Clio, the Muse of History, in her chariot, notes significant events as they transpire. The clock was once the official timepiece of the House.

In 1829 Andrew Jackson was inaugurated as the seventh President of the United States on the East Front steps of the Capitol. This event was captured in a painting by artist Allyn Cox in the first floor corridor of the House Wing (1974).

The House of Representatives had its own characters in those lively years. One of the best-remembered was John Randolph of Virginia, a member of the famous family that provided both the Old Dominion and the United States with a number of outstanding public servants. John Randolph served in the House and Senate almost continuously from 1799 until his death in 1833, but his first love was always hunting. At the height of the hunting season, it was his regular practice to ride to the hounds from dawn until the hour the House's session began. At the appointed time, he would gallop to the Capitol; "leaving his lathered horse with grooms, Randolph would then stride into the House Chamber, still clothed in mud-spattered boots and red hunting coat, with a pack of hounds padding along at his heels".

During those years the atmosphere within the grand space of the Rotunda was also far different from its present august dignity. Numerous vendors hawked items ranging from food to souvenirs. Petitioners and office-seekers trailed Congressmen as they moved in and out of the legislative chambers and committee rooms. Temporary exhibits displaying the latest innovations in science, agriculture, or industry attracted various passers-by. In both House and Senate restaurants, refreshments were liberally and regularly enjoyed by thirsty legislators, despite the fact that the American Congressional Temperance Society had been established in the House Chamber itself in 1833. A few years later, the Senate voted to ban the sale of hard liquor in the Capitol. The House refused to go along, and for seven years, the Senate abided by its own resolution while the other side of the building continued to flow with strong drink.

The most pervasive habit of the time, if we are to accept accounts of contemporary European travelers in America, was the use of tobacco in the form of chewing or snuff. Both men and women seem to have enjoyed those forms of tobacco. Charles Dickens wrote: "Washington may be called the headquarters of tobacco tinctured saliva . . . In all public places of America, this filthy custom is recognized."

One thing foreign visitors did agree upon was the grandeur of the Capitol itself. Mrs. Frances Trollope, an English visitor noted for her acid pen, appeared to be happily surprised by the building:

"Our first object the next morning was to get sight of the Capitol, and our impatience sent us forth before breakfast. The mists of morning still hung around this magnificent building when first it broke upon our view, and I am not sure that the effect produced was not the greater for this circumstance. At all events, we were struck with admiration and surprise. None of us, I believe, expected to see so imposing a structure on that side of the Atlantic. I am ill at describing buildings, but the beauty and majesty of the American capitol might defy an abler pen than mine to do it justice. It stands so finely too, high, and alone.

" The magnificent western facade is approached from the city by terraces and steps of bolder proportions than I ever before saw. The elegant eastern front, to which many persons give the preference, is on a level with a newly-planted, but exceedingly handsome enclosure, which in a few years, will offer the shade of all the most splendid trees which flourish in the Union. . . ."

The Capitol was the scene of many "firsts" in American history. In 1829, in a ceremony open to the public, Andrew Jackson became the first President to be inaugurated on the East Front steps. Until that time, chief executives had been installed either in the Senate or House of Representatives' Chamber, with only invited guests being admitted. Old Hickory would have none of that; he had been elected as a man of the people and he was determined to have his installation open to everyone. Six years later, President Jackson was the first victim of an assassination attempt at the Capitol. On January 30, 1835, Jackson attended funeral services in the Capitol. As he was leaving the Rotunda to return to the White House, a man accosted him, raised a pistol, and fired point blank at the President. The weapon misfired; Jackson, no stranger to a good scuffle, went after the would-be assassin with his cane. A second pistol also misfired, and the President and a navy lieutenant succeeded in disarming the assailant.

John Quincy Adams has the distinction of being one of two Presidents who were elected to Congress after leaving the White House. The other, Andrew Johnson, was elected to the Senate but served only a short time before his death. Adams continued to serve with great distinction for seventeen years; he was stricken on the floor of the House in 1848 while delivering an impassioned attack on the treaty which had just ended the Mexican War. The old warrior was carried from the floor to the Speaker's office, where he died two days later. A bronze disc was set into the floor of the old House Chamber to mark the site of his desk. It remains today, not only as a tribute to Adams, but also to mark the famous "whispering spot", where words spoken softly can be heard all the way across the room.

The Capitol is seldom thought of as a scientific laboratory, but it was there in 1844 that Samuel F. B. Morse first demonstrated the telegraph in the Old Supreme Court Chamber. Forty miles of wire had been strung to Baltimore, where his assistant waited with a receiving set. Morse tapped out the historic message: "What hath God wrought?" From Baltimore Morse's assistant stoically flashed in return, "What is the news in Washington?"

By the eighteen-forties, it was apparent that Congress was outgrowing the Capitol. When Dr. Thornton had submitted his design in 1792, the Senate consisted of 30 Members, and the House 106. The results of the 1850 census caused the House to be enlarged to 232 Members, and the 31 States of the Union sent 62 Senators to Washington. Thus Congress had more than doubled, and the country had spread across the continent. It was obvious that the Capitol would have to be enlarged; Senator Jefferson Davis of Mississippi, who became President of the Confederacy, served as a persuasive spokesman for those Members of both Houses favoring expansion. In September 1850, Congress appropriated funds for design and construction of two large new wings. The architect chosen for the new wings was Thomas U. Walter of Philadelphia, who was already supervising

In 1835, after attending the funeral for a Member of Congress, President Andrew Jackson was rushed on the steps of the Capitol by a would-be assassin. The President escaped death because both guns of the attacker misfired.

The Old Supreme Court Chamber probably appeared much like this restored view when Morse demonstrated his invention to Congress.

Robert Mills, architect of the Treasury Building and the Washington Monument, was an unsuccessful competitor for the 1850 Extension project. This view from the Senate end of the Capitol shows his idea for a dome.

construction of the Treasury Building near the White House. Massachusetts and Maryland marble were selected for construction of the new wings in place of the Virginia sandstone used in the old Capitol. The official cornerstone-laying for the new wings occurred on July 4, 1851, when President Millard Fillmore presided over the ceremony wearing the same Masonic apron that President Washington had used six decades earlier. But the real highlight of the day was the principal address delivered by old "Black Dan" himself, Daniel Webster. Webster, then Secretary of State, had spent most of the previous thirty years in the House and Senate. Against the background of worsening relations between the North and South, Webster's speech became a plea for the preservation of the Union. Of the three former rhetorical "giants" of the Senate, Calhoun was dead, Clay was near the end of his brilliant career, and Webster himself was in the final year of his life.

If the future of the Republic seemed in doubt, that of the Capitol was not. Thomas Walter pressed ahead with the new Senate and House wings; by late 1857, the House of Representatives moved into its new Chamber, and in January of 1859, the Senate occupied the north wing, although much embellishment and decorative work remained to be done. It had been apparent almost from the beginning of the expansion that despite the intentional visual harmony of the new and old sections, the Bulfinch dome was dwarfed by the bulk of the enlarged Capitol. The decision was made to replace the dome with one more proportionate to the whole structure, one which was in fact nearly twice as high as the old Bulfinch dome. Walter drew on elements present in several of the great domes of the Old World—for example, St. Peter's in Rome and St. Paul's in London—to produce the masterpiece that today is instantly recognizable world-wide.

Secretary of War Jefferson Davis objected to the statue planned to surmount the dome, an allegorical female figure representing "Freedom"; in early models she wore a liberty cap derived in form from antique classical models and associated with freedom from slavery. Davis argued from the Southern point of view that such a depiction would only further inflame the pro- and anti-slavery passions that were sweeping the country in the mid-nineteenth century, and so Thomas Crawford, the sculptor, altered his design, substituting a helmet

Thomas U. Walter, the fourth Architect of the Capitol, was originally hired as the Architect of the Extension. This 1851 elevation shows the proposed new House and Senate Wings. The Bulfinch dome is still visible in this drawing.

Daniel Webster delivered a two hour oration at the Corner Stone Laying Ceremony for the Extension in 1851.

Influence of classic architecture on U.S. Capitol. (L. to R.) St. Pauls Cathedral, London; U.S. Capitol; St. Peters Cathedral, Rome; all drawn to same scale. The grandeur of the two cathedral domes undoubtedly influenced Thomas U. Walter's design for the dome of our Capitol.

ST. PAUL   U.S. CAPITOL   ST. PETER

surmounted by an eagle's head and feathers, and encircled with stars.

Crawford's statue of "Freedom" was fortunate to arrive in America at all. The sculptor modeled the statue in his studio in Rome; in April, 1858, his full-size plaster model was shipped from Leghorn, Italy for casting in America. The boat carrying the statue was so old and slow that it took a full month to cross the Mediterranean, and even then was forced to put in at Gibraltar for the repair of her many leaks. After a month in Gibraltar, the ship sailed again for New York, and this time made it as far as Bermuda, where the leaks were judged so extensive that the ship was pronounced a total loss and sold. It was not until December, 1858, that "Freedom" arrived in New York, and it was to be another five years before she was cast in bronze and placed on the tholos of the Capitol dome.

The enlarged Capitol offered legislators a luxury of space on a scale that was not possible in the old building. Ample offices were provided for principal officers of both Houses, while comfortable lobbies were included for the relaxation of Senators and Representatives. Another innovation in 1859 was the installation of marble bathtubs. In the days when many Senators and Representatives lived in rooming houses and hotels that boasted few amenities, the handsome marble tubs, located in the Capitol basement, provided a popular service. Two are left,

This is a rare photograph of a detail of Thomas Crawford's "Freedom". Commissioned in 1856, the statue was raised into place on top of the dome in 1863.

The Senate Marble Room is one of Thomas U. Walter's most luxurious interior spaces. The room is so named because it is constructed from floor to ceiling in marble.

Nineteenth century ornateness characterizes the Senate Reception Room. Here Senators meet their constituents and guests from home.

Architect's model. Architect Thomas Walter's sketch in 1860 shows him judging elevation and profiles.

Cross-section of the dome. This projection was prepared in 1857.

The dome evolves. Drawing of the dome as accepted.

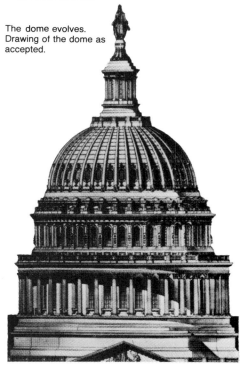

The Hall of Columns is located on the first floor of the House Wing. The marble and bronze statues are part of the National Statuary Hall Collection.

The assault on Senator Sumner by a Member of the House of Representatives is depicted in this 1856 edition of "Frank Leslie's Illustrated Newspaper".

but they are in unusable condition in a basement office used by Senate engineers.

During the eighteen-fifties, the argument over slavery grew in intensity, and Daniel Webster's worst fears were borne out. Congress had always been "rough-and-tumble"; Vice President Martin Van Buren had occasionally worn a brace of pistols thrust in his belt while presiding over the Senate. Tempers flared frequently, and a Senator from South Carolina wrote that "every man on the floor of both Houses is armed with a revolver". On May 20, 1856, Senator Charles Sumner of Massachusetts rose to denounce Senator A. P. Butler's stand on the Kansas-Nebraska Act, which had repealed the Missouri Compromise and instead made it theoretically possible for the Nebraska Territory to enter the Union as a slave State. He characterized Senator Butler, an aging South Carolinian, as a Don Quixote who had made vows to a mistress who, "though polluted in the sight of the world, is chaste in his sight. I mean the harlot, slavery". Two days later, in the nearly empty chamber, Sumner was approached at his desk by Representative Preston Brooks of South Carolina, a kinsman of Senator Butler. Brooks said, "I have read your speech twice over carefully; it is a libel on South Carolina, and Mr. Butler, who is a relative of mine." Without another word, Brooks began to beat Senator Sumner with his heavy, metal-capped walking stick. Brooks continued to strike the Massachusetts Senator until he fell unconscious. Sumner's injuries were so severe that it was several years before he could return to his duties.

The inevitable rupture came in 1861, when Senators and Representatives from States which had seceded resigned from Congress and left Washington. When the first influx of volunteers from the northeastern States began to pour into Washington, troops were billeted in the Capitol, since Congress was not in session at the time. A bakery was established in the basement to feed the Union troops their daily ten-ounce bread ration. President Lincoln had originally asked for 75,000 volunteers willing to serve for ninety days, but it soon became apparent that the war would be a long and hard-fought struggle. The carefree young men who had camped out in the Rotunda were molded into hardened soldiers by the time the Second Battle of Manassas and the Battle of Antietam were fought in 1862. Thousands of wounded men from the two engagements spilled into Washington, filling the Army hospitals which had been established in public buildings. In the midst of the emergency, the Capitol was again employed: fifteen hundred cots were set up in its great open spaces, and they were quickly filled with wounded soldiers.

Numerous anecdotes are preserved which reflect the intense emotions of this period. Early in the conflict, a Union Army private mounting guard at the Capitol was shown the Senate Chamber desk occupied by Senator Jefferson Davis in the years before the war. In an outburst of frustrated rage, he thrust his bayonet deeply into the dark mahogany desk. The damage has long since been skillfully repaired.

Throughout these trying months, work on the great cast iron dome had gone ahead under Thomas Walter's direction. Colonel Montgomery Meigs, Chief of the Army Corps of Engineers, had halted construction for a short time during the summer of 1861, but President Lincoln's personal determination to see the Capitol completed had prevailed. He was once asked by a visitor, John Eaton of Ohio, how he could justify the continued construction of the building, especially of the cast iron dome. Lincoln calmly replied that the work must continue. "If the people see the Capitol going on, it is a sign that we intend the Union shall go on." In late 1863, the President must have felt supremely vindicated: that year brought victories at Vicksburg and Gettysburg which pointed the way to ultimate triumph for the Union. On December 2nd, while he himself lay in bed with a fever, a huge crowd gathered in the Capitol Plaza to watch while the sections of Thomas Crawford's statue of "Freedom" were raised to the summit of the dome and bolted together. Upon the completion of the task, a tremendous salute was sounded from the guns of the thirty-six surrounding forts that protected Washington.

During the Civil War the Rotunda became a field hospital. Work on the dome was halted for a while but the elaborate scaffolding needed for its construction was left in place. Allyn Cox recorded this moment as part of the decorations for the House corridor (1974).

This 1863 drawing by Architect Walter shows the head of Thomas Crawford's "Freedom" being raised into place atop the new cast iron dome.

During the Civil War parts of the Capitol were used for the troops. In this view supplies are shown stored under the Senate Chamber while bread ovens were in rooms on the basement floor.

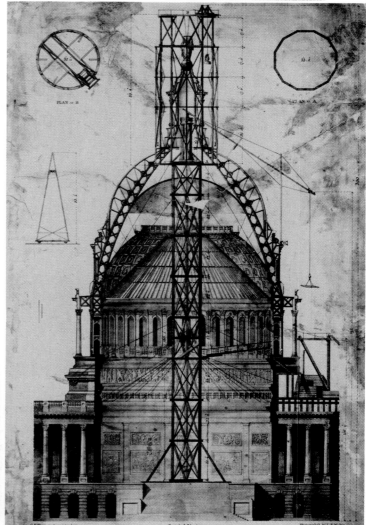

The Capitol in Various Stages of Growth

Early photograph of the Capitol, about 1850. Note the tiny wrought iron balcony on the Senate side. A connecting corridor and the present Senate wing now obliterate this view of the original north wing.

New Senate wing nearly completed, the House wing and the dome still under construction. In May 1861 the "Illustrated London News" carried this woodcut. It was slightly in advance of the actual progress as the Senate steps and portico had not progressed this far. Tiber Creek runs down the mall toward the half completed Washington Monument.

House wing under construction. With the extension of the building it was necessary to remove the iron Bulfinch gates and enlarge the grounds. Three of the supporting square posts are now located on Constitution Avenue.

The Capitol, 1861. Less than a month after Lincoln was inaugurated the first time, the Civil War broke out and troops were called to protect the Capitol. Statuary for the Senate pediment and troops drilling on the east lawn were all part of the Capitol scene this May day of 1861.

By sailboat to the Capitol in 1860. From the White House side or mall end this was the scene more than 100 years ago, showing the old canal and the Botanic Garden.

A marble monolithic column for the Senate portico is swung into place. In the background the dome nears completion.

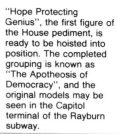

"Hope Protecting Genius", the first figure of the House pediment, is ready to be hoisted into position. The completed grouping is known as "The Apotheosis of Democracy", and the original models may be seen in the Capitol terminal of the Rayburn subway.

Horsecars at the Capitol (Summer 1862). The horsecar line ran across the east plaza. Blocks of marble are visible in the foreground but construction is completed.

Pediment of the House wing nears completion. The sculptural work by Paul W. Bartlett was authorized in 1908 and the unveiling ceremony took place in 1916. Here craftsmen are about to put another allegorical figure into position.

Capitol Interiors

In 1864 the Congress came up with the answer to one of the most annoying problems raised by the enlargement of the Capitol, the question of what was to be done with the Old House Chamber. The Senate had previously reassigned its former quarters to the Supreme Court, which occupied the former Senate Chamber until 1935. The House Chamber was another matter: it was too large to be used for any subsidiary function, too handsome a room to subdivide into office space, and traffic between the House and Senate Wings passed directly through it. After 1857, the House almost seemed to forget its existence, and the Chamber fell into disuse and disrepair. Old funiture, boxes, bales and other unwanted material were stored in its corners. In 1864, Representative Justin Morrill, author of the Morrill Act which provided for land grant colleges, rose in the House to offer a solution to the dilemma: "To what end more useful or grand, and at the same time simple and inexpensive, can we devote it [the old Chamber] than to ordain that it shall be set apart for the reception of such statuary as each State shall elect to be deserving of this lasting commemoration?" His proposal became law on July 2, 1864, and thus the

The original House of Representatives Chamber was restored to some of its 1822 splendor during 1976. The Chamber became Statuary Hall in 1864.

Statuary Hall was born. A statue of Rhode Island's fighting Quaker general of the Revolution, Nathanael Greene, was the first to be placed in the Hall.

In time, there came to be almost a forest of statues of every size in the Hall, and in the early 1930s, engineers discovered that their enormous weight was endangering the structure of the floor, the Hall being in one of the oldest parts of the building. In 1933, provision was made for relocation of as many statues as necessary to relieve pressure on the foundation. Statuary Hall did not change substantially again until the 1970s, when Congress decided to restore, insofar as possible, the room to its original appearance as the House Chamber. A number of statues were relocated, and the remainder rearranged in a more attractive pattern. The handsome half-dome that had replaced the original was decorated, the walls cleaned, and replicas of the original bronze chandelier and sconces installed. Heavy scarlet brocade draperies, reproductions of the originals, were hung in the old visitors' gallery. Duplicates of the original fireplace mantels and two ornately carved frames holding engraved copies of the Declaration of Independence were also placed in the Chamber.

Much of the Capitol's greatest interior decorative art was completed during a twenty-five year period by Constantino Brumidi, a talented painter and muralist who fled political persecution in his native Italy, arriving in the United States in 1852. In 1855 he began the embellishment of the United States Capitol; his legacy includes the corridors of the Senate Wing, the formal offices of the President and Vice President, the Senate Reception Room, the present House and Senate Appropriations Committees rooms, and most important, his work in the Rotunda. In 1877, when he was seventy-two years old, Brumidi began his last work, the fresco

Before Brumidi began painting the frieze in the Capitol, he rendered a 24 foot preliminary drawing. The section of it shown depicts "Pizarro's Conquest of Peru, 1533".

The elaborate corridor paintings in the Senate Wing are the work of Constantino Brumidi.

Everyday the Rotunda fills with thousands of visitors interested in the art and history of the building.

Originally, a grand staircase was planned for this space. After the fire of 1814, Latrobe abandoned that idea and constructed a small rotunda inside the existing oval space.

frieze encircling the top of the Rotunda. Its subjects include various epic events in American history, such as the landing of Columbus, William Penn's treaty with the Indians, the great battles of the Revolution, and the discovery of gold in California. Brumidi had completed about one quarter of the work when his scaffold slipped. He managed to save himself by clinging onto the platform for 20 minutes until help came, but the shock was so great that he was never able to return to his work. He died three months later in February 1880. During the following eight years, Filippo Costaggini completed the great frieze using Brumidi's cartoons, except for a thirty-two foot gap that was completed by Allyn Cox in 1953. Brumidi's great wish, which he once expressed in a letter, was "that I may live long enough to make beautiful the Capitol of the one country on earth in which there is liberty". Every visitor to the Capitol sees the evidence of his success.

Throughout the latter half of the century, numerous conveniences were installed in the Capitol. Plumbing, steam heat, and forced air ventilation were introduced by 1865; the first elevators went into operation in 1874; the building was more adequately fireproofed in 1881; and by 1900 the Capitol was completely wired for electricity. The engineers in charge of planning the new plumbing system were appalled at the condition of the old water closet drains: they claimed the build-up of sewer gas was so great that a single spark could have touched off a massive explosion. As a byproduct of the modernization process, the Capitol did lose some of its romance; one by one its fireplaces were walled up or removed, until now there are few that are operable. The chimneys remain, however: there are no fewer than one hundred and thirtynine on the roof.

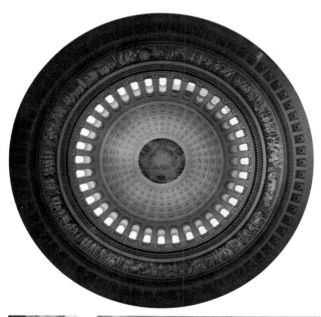

The huge windows in the giant dome help create the illusion of a "floating dome".

The walls of Senate corridors are part of an elaborate decorative scheme developed and executed by Constantino Brumidi.

The Speaker's Lobby is located behind the House of Representatives Chamber. After a Speaker of the House retires, his portrait is hung in this area of the Capitol.

One Nation Under God, Indivisible

Reverend Edward L. R. Elson, Chaplain of the U.S. Senate, left, and Reverend James D. Ford, Chaplain of the U.S. House of Representatives.

The first act which really united all the American colonists into one people was the first Continental Day of Prayer. By a resolution on June 12, 1775, the Second Continental Congress summoned the "inhabitants of all the English colonies on this continent to a day of fasting and prayer" on Thursday, July 20, 1775, to "confess . . . our many sins; and offer . . . supplications to the all-wise, omnipotent, and merciful Disposer of all events . . .". When July 20th came, the Congress set the example for the people. In the morning the Members assembled in their hall, then walked as a body four blocks to Christ Church where they not only prayed but also heard a sermon. That night, they repeated their morning action by walking to the First Presbyterian Church where they prayed and listened to another sermon. It is recorded that about two million of the nearly three million people in the Thirteen Colonies kept the fast and prayed in their churches and homes on this Day of Prayer. One historian wrote that this was the day the colonies became one nation. Since that day there have been more than one hundred ninety officially proclaimed National Days of Prayer.

The President is authorized to proclaim at least two National Days of Prayer each year. Public Law 82–324 requires the President to proclaim a National Day of Prayer on a day other than a Sunday. Under Public Law 77–379 the President proclaims the fourth Thursday of November each year as a National Day of Thanksgiving. Other national observances such as Memorial Day and Veterans Day are reverently observed with prayers of thanksgiving and supplications for God's guidance.

On September 7, 1774, nearly two years before the Declaration of Independence, the Reverend Jacob Duchè offered the first prayer in the Continental Congress. Since then prayer has been offered regularly in Congress. When the Constitution was adopted and the First Congress convened in April, 1789, among the first officers elected in the Senate and the House of Representatives were the chaplains who opened each day's session with prayer and performed other religious functions. Similarly, when the Supreme Court convenes and the black robed Chief Justice and Associate Justices stand before their desks, the Marshal makes an ascription to Almighty God in the Court Call saying, "God save the United States and this honorable court."

Flag Day, June 14, 1954, President Dwight D. Eisenhower stood on the steps of the Capitol Building and with his fellow citizens, for the first time, recited the revised pledge to the flag which by Public Law 83–396 henceforth would include the phrase, "one nation under God".

This pledge attests what has been true about America from the beginning. Faith in the transcendent, sovereign God was in the public philosophy—the American consensus. America's story opens with the first words of the Bible, "In the beginning God . . .". "We are truthfully one nation 'under God' and our institutions 'presuppose a Divine Being'" wrote Associate Justice William O. Douglas in 1966. Only a nation founded on theistic pre-suppositions would adopt a first amendment to ensure the free exercise of all religions or of none. The government would be neutral among the many denominations and no one church would become "the state church". But America and its institutions of government could not be neutral about God.

It is appropriate, then, that in the Capitol Building a room was set aside by the Eighty-third Congress to be used exclusively for the private prayer and meditation of Members of Congress. No sectarian liturgical services may be held here and it is not open to the public. But while the Congress is at work the Prayer Room is open so that individual Senators and Representatives may enter this quiet place to renew their spiritual and intellectual powers.

The history that gives this room its inspirational lift is centered in the stained glass window. George Washington kneeling in prayer, against a background of ruby glass imported from England, France and Germany, is the focus of the composition. The phrase *"E Pluribus Unum"* conveys the meaning of America. In religion it signifies America's faith in tolerance and mutual respect. In statecraft it signified then one Nation out of Thirteen Colonies, today one Nation out of fifty States and possessions; and it signifies one people. The window itself is an anonymous gift from a group of designers and craftsmen in California's 21st Congressional District as a "thank offering to this country".

The larger glass area of the window came from West Virginia and Indiana. Behind Washington a prayer is etched: "Preserve me, O God, for in Thee do I put my trust", the first verse of the sixteenth Psalm.

There are upper and lower medallions representing the two sides of the Great Seal of the United States. On these are inscribed the phrases: *annuit coeptis*—"God has favored our undertakings"—and *novus ordo seclorum*—"A new order of the ages is born." Under the upper medallion is the phrase from Lincoln's immortal Gettysburg Address, "This Nation under God". The names of the thirteen original States are on scrolls in the central portion, each with its star nearby. The names of the other States in chronological order are on the laurel leaf border. The two lower corners of the window each show the Holy Scriptures, an open book and a candle, signifying the light from God's law, "Thy Word is a lamp unto my feet and a light unto my path."

On the altar are two vases filled with fresh flowers. At the right and left are two candelabra, each with the traditional seven lights. An American flag is at the right of the altar. In front of each candelabrum is a prie-dieu or prayer bench where those who desire to do so may kneel. The bench cushions are covered with needlepoint made by wives of Congressmen. Ten chairs face the central window. The walls are pastel green; the ceiling displays the original painting, with cloud panels trimmed with gold. The altar and prayer benches are of white oak.

When illuminated by the indirect light from the shielded wall brackets, the room is a soft color harmony of green and gold.

Neither large enough nor designed for a religious assembly, it is adequate for its avowed purpose—a shrine at which the Nation's lawmakers may worship God, each in his or her own way.

Prayer Room
for Members of Congress

Capitol Landscape and Improvements

Frederick L. Olmsted was hired by the Senate Committee on Buildings and Grounds in 1874 to landscape the Capitol campus. This master plan also shows an extension on the Capitol to the West that was being planned concurrently.

During the years 1865 through 1900, the Capitol's natural surroundings began to acquire the grace and dignity they retain today. When the Capitol was built, the Grounds were planted in a rural, informal manner. One writer described the soil at that time as being "exceedingly stiff clay, becoming dust in dry and mortar in rainy weather". Only four decades later, however, Mrs. Trollope, the English chronicler, called the Grounds an "exceedingly handsome enclosure",

and accurately predicted that "in a few years, [they] will offer the shade of all the most splendid trees which flourish in the Union". Today, after several annexations, they comprise a remarkable green oasis in the city. Tourists enjoy them, and Congressional employees relax under the great trees during their lunch hours. The Capitol Grounds comprise 181 acres today, and contain more than one hundred species of plants, shrubs, and trees, including the symbolic gifts of State trees from thirty-three States of the Union. The native species of the Eastern United States predominate, with nine varieties of maple and elm, and twelve of oak; also planted on the Grounds is a giant sequoia, the king of trees, a gift of the State of California.

Not until 1874 were the Capitol Grounds embellished by the master landscaper whose work is still abundantly evident to us today. Frederick Law Olmsted, the greatest landscape

General Plan for the Improvement of the U.S. Capitol Grounds.

Tulips in bloom on the West Front of the Capitol.

Aerial view of West Front of the Capitol with Senate Office Buildings, Supreme Court and Library of Congress in background.

The West Front of the Capitol once overlooked marshland, a canal and a railroad station. The Olmsted grounds (1880's) and the design of the Mall (early 20th century) provided the green areas known today.

This print from a drawing by Hughson Hawley was done around the turn of the century. It shows the new Olmsted terraces and an Edward Clark proposal for the construction of a pediment and large portico on the West Front.

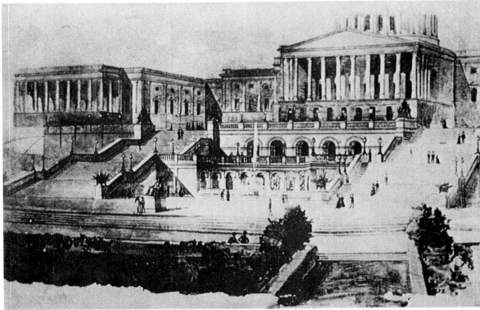

Cameron Elm, circa 1920.

architect in America, came to Washington fresh from his triumph in New York City, where he planned Central Park. Arriving in the Federal City, he remarked that the Capitol Grounds were in a state of "sylvan juvenility", and he immediately set to work planning the graceful plantings and walks that have delighted visitors ever since. Mr. Olmsted recognized that the soil of the Capitol Grounds was too impoverished to support the extensive plantings he recommended, so his first task was to improve its fertility. His work crews plowed and drained the soil, dressed it with oyster-shell lime and swamp muck, exposed the mix to a winter's frosts, and then topped it all off with a compost of manure and more swamp muck, a necessary process, but one which also must surely have brought a pungent aroma to Capitol Hill during the warm summer months. Olmsted's plans were warmly received by Congress, but on one occasion he found his grand scheme supplanted by the desires of the Senate. One morning in 1875, Senator Simon Cameron of Pennsylvania was crossing the Grounds on his way to the Capitol when he saw a work crew preparing to chop down an ancient and majestic elm near the House which stood in the way of one of Mr. Olmsted's proposed promenades. Senator Cameron demanded that the workmen stop, and then ran to the Senate Chamber, where his fellow Members had already begun their session. Begging the floor from the Senator who was speaking at the time, he rose and asked the Senate to express its opinion that the handsome and venerable elm ought to be spared. The tree flourishes today near the House entrance; it has, in fact, been named the "Cameron Elm" in honor of its savior.

Vice President James S. Sherman planting a tree on the Senate side of the Capitol on April 18, 1912.

Olmsted's work at the Capitol was not confined to landscaping. He was also responsible for the design of a very prominent part of the Capitol's structure: the graceful and dignified West Front terraces which replaced Bulfinch's earthen terraces of 1829. He also designed and erected a rocky grotto on the Senate side of the Grounds with spring water piped in from the northern section of the city; it has served as a shady retreat for generations of visitors. Yet even as Olmsted proceeded with his work, there were occasional reminders that elegant landscaping and terraces could not change the fact that Washington was still a small city. A routine report filed in 1877, at the height of Mr. Olmsted's activity, recommended that Congress make a special appropriation to replace tender shrubbery and young trees damaged by the cattle that wandered onto the Capitol Grounds.

Early in the twentieth century, the Capitol was joined on the summit of Capitol Hill by two office buildings, one for each House. The Capitol had become uncomfortably overcrowded, and the two new structures were needed to accommodate a Congress grown to four hundred and thirty-five Representatives and ninety-six Senators. The House office building was later named for the late Speaker Joseph Cannon, and that of the Senate for the late Richard Russell of Georgia.

Two additional House office buildings, named for the late Speakers Nicholas Longworth and Sam Rayburn, as well as a second building for the Senate, the Everett Dirksen Senate Office Building, named for the late great orator from Illinois, have also been constructed. Currently under way is an addition to the Dirksen Building, which will be named in honor of the late Senator Philip Hart of Michigan.

Longworth House Office Building

Cannon House Office Building

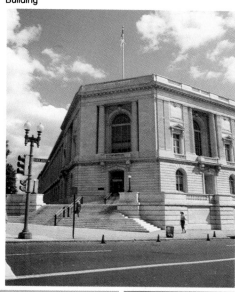

Rayburn House Office Building

Russell Senate Office Building

Dirksen Senate Office Building

Improvements within the Capitol Building itself have also continued throughout this century. In 1929, Congress authorized the installation of air conditioning, then a radical innovation, in the Capitol and the House and Senate Office Buildings. When the Capitol Power Plant was completed three years later, it was the largest air conditioning unit in the world. The year 1958 saw the beginning of construction on the largest modification made to the Capitol since Thomas Walter's dome was finished in 1863. Over the years, the aging sandstone East Front of the Capitol had seriously deteriorated. During the following four years a new front, duplicating the old front but extending it by thirty-two feet, was constructed from marble; this new addition provided space for offices and public rooms. The extension was a fulfillment of the intention of Walter's original plans of 1874. From the time he designed the House and Senate wings in the 1850s, he had urged for the sake of proportion that the East Front be extended.

Gardens above the House garage.

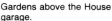

30

Visitors to the Capitol in the Bicentennial Year found the building more beautiful than ever; the interior was cleaned and repainted, and the Old Supreme Court, Senate Chamber, and Statuary Hall were restored. In the ground floor of the House Wing, artist Allyn Cox finished a spectacular series of murals depicting the many meeting places of Congress and great moments in the history of the Capitol. The project must have seemed like a nostalgic homecoming to Mr. Cox: he had worked in the Capitol once before, in the 1950s, when he completed Constantino Brumidi's Rotunda frieze.

Congressman Frank Thompson, Jr. (right), of New Jersey, Chairman, Committee on House Administration and George White (left), Architect of the Capitol with artist Allyn Cox.

Senate side of Capitol at night.

West Front of Capitol and reflecting pool.

Repairs to sidewalk on the East Front of Capitol.

The Capitol from Senate side.

Perhaps the highlight of the Bicentennial year in the United States Capitol came on June 3rd, when one of the four extant copies of the original draft of the Magna Carta went on temporary display in the Rotunda, part of Great Britain's participation in the two hundredth anniversary of America's freedom. Magna Carta was the first great step taken toward establishing limited governments designated to protect the freedom of a country's citizens, rather than to deprive them of it. It is fitting that the exhibition in the Rotunda took place in the building that is the political heart of the Nation that guarantees liberty for all its people, the United States Capitol.

The Old Supreme Court Chamber was restored to include furnishings from its inception to 1860. This project, directed by George M. White, Architect of the Capitol, was completed in 1976.

The original Senate Chamber was restored in 1976. The mid-nineteenth century furnishings remind one of the days of eloquence of Webster, Clay and Calhoun.

Magna Carta on display in the Capitol Rotunda during the Bicentennial.

First floor passageway before remodeling. This area was constructed when an interior courtyard was converted into office space in 1901.

First floor passageway after modification. The octagonal shape of the above passageway is repeated in the same materials with a variation in the floor and ceiling design.

Second floor passageway before reconstruction. The passage was constructed in 1901. At that time, the walls were covered in white glazed brick.

Second floor passageway after modification. Caen stone walls, octagonal marble floor, ornamental plaster ceiling and appropriate chandelier embellish the space.

These award winning extreme wide angle photographs capture the dramatic designs of Benjamin H. Latrobe, Second Architect of the Capitol. The photo at left is the stairwell on the House side of the Capitol at the eastern side of the building. The Senate companion area is shown at the right. Latrobe planned these powerful, elegant and essential staircases after the catastrophic fire of 1814. Photographs by Harry L. Burnett, Jr. of the Architect's Office.

Memorial and Historic Trees on the United States Capitol Grounds

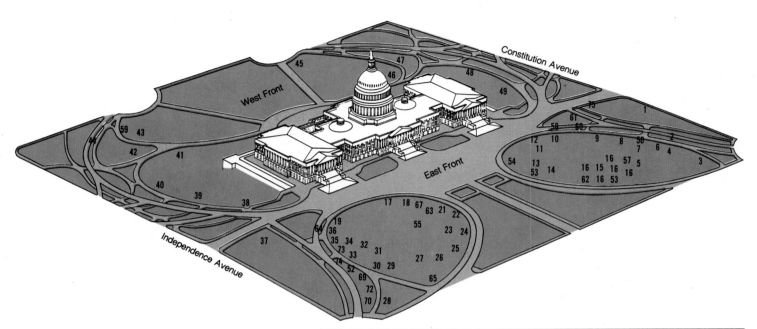

Since the early 1900s, ninety–four memorial and historic trees have been planted with seventy–three still living on the Capitol Grounds—this chart and guide will help to locate them.

* Memorial or historic tree which has been removed from the Capitol Grounds.
** Memorial or historic tree located in the courtyard of the Everett McKinley Dirksen Office Building.
*** Memorial or historic trees located in the lower West Court Terrace of the Rayburn House Office Building.

Key No.	Date planted	Planted by or memorializing	State	Common name of tree	Botanical name of tree
*	Prior to 1800	George Washington	Virginia	American Elm	*Ulmus americana.*
38	Prior to 1875	Senator Simon D. Cameron	Pennsylvania	American Elm	*Ulmus americana.*
*	April 18, 1912	Vice President James S. Sherman	New York	Purple Beech	*Fagus sylvatica.*
*	April 24, 1912	Senator Augustus O. Bacon	Georgia	Pin Oak	*Quercus palustris.*
44	April 24, 1912	Representative William J. Browning	New Jersey	Red Oak	*Quercus borealis.*
2	April 30, 1912	Senator Jacob H. Gallinger	New Hampshire	Overcup Oak	*Quercus lyrata.*
*	May 4, 1912	Senator Henry C. Lodge, Sr.	Massachusetts	Red Oak	*Quercus borealis.*
18	May 4, 1912	Representative James R. Mann	Illinois	Red Oak	*Quercus borealis.*
19	May 7, 1912	Speaker Champ Clark	Missouri	Sugar Maple	*Acer saccharum.*
4	May 9, 1912	Senator Shelby M. Cullom	Illinois	American Elm	*Ulmus americana.*
*	May 11, 1912	Senator George P. Wetmore	Rhode Island	American Beech	*Fagus americana.*
*	April 21, 1913	Representative Richard Bartholdt (Peace Tree)	Missouri	Pin Oak	*Quercus palustris.*
41	1913	Representative Marlin E. Olmsted	Pennsylvania	Pin Oak	*Quercus palustris.*
34	1913	Speaker Joseph G. Cannon	Illinois	Red Oak	*Quercus borealis.*
33	1916 or 1917	Representative Joseph Taggart	Kansas	Pin Oak	*Quercus palustris.*

Key No.	Date planted	Planted by or memorializing	State	Common name of tree	Botanical name of tree
*	1917 or 1918	Representative Jeannette Rankin	Montana	Redwood	*Sequoia gigantea.*
8	April 8, 1918	Vice President Thomas R. Marshall	Indiana	Hickory	*Hicoria alba.*
13	April 8, 1918	Senator Willard Saulsbury	Delaware	Hickory	*Hicoria alba.*
*	1918 or 1919	Representative James L. Slayden	Texas	Pecan	*Hicoria pecan.*
42	1918 or 1919	Representative James L. Slayden	Texas	Pecan	*Hicoria pecan.*
39	1920	Representative Charles H. Randall	California	Redwood	*Sequoia gigantea.*
17	April 15, 1920	Representative Joseph Walsh	Massachusetts	American Beech	*Fagus grandiflora.*
*	April 20, 1923	Senator Charles L. McNary	Oregon	Red Oak	*Quercus borealis.*
*	May 9, 1925	Mothers' Tree (planted to honor Mothers of America)	All States	White Birch	*Betula laciniata.*
*	Nov. 23, 1927	Representative Martin B. Madden	Illinois	Mossycup Oak	*Quercus macrocarpa.*
40	Nov. 26, 1927	Representative David H. Kincheloe	Kentucky	Umbrella Tree	*Magnolia tripetala.*
*	May 4, 1928	Representative Roy G. Fitzgerald	Ohio	Bullbay Tree	*Magnolia grandiflora.*
*	1929–1933	Vice President Charles Curtis	Kansas	Bullbay Tree	*Magnolia grandiflora.*
*	May 1929	Senator Simeon D. Fess	Ohio	Buckeye	*Aesculus glabra.*
*	April 20, 1931	Boy Scout Tree (from Mount Vernon, Va.) First step in nut tree planting program	Virginia	White Walnut	*Juglans cinerea.*
*	Dec. 21, 1931	Scion of Washington Elm (from Washington State)	Washington	American Elm	*Ulmus americana.*
*	Dec. 21, 1931	Representative Maurice H. Thatcher	Kentucky	American Elm	*Ulmus americana.*
28	April 22, 1932	To honor 100th anniversary of the birth of J. Sterling Morton, founder of Arbor Day; and bicentennial of George Washington	Virginia	Black Walnut	*Juglans nigra.*
30	April 8, 1936	J. Sterling Morton Tree (Representative Karl Stefan, sponsor)	Nebraska	White Pine	*Pinus strobus.*
*	Nov. 9, 1939	Sam Houston Centennial Tree (replanted by Fritz G. Lanham)	Texas	Pecan	*Hicoria pecan.*
15	May 30, 1946	War Memorial Tree (Representative John E. Rankin, sponsor)	All States	White Oak	*Quercus alba.*
6	April 10, 1947	Arbor Day Tree—75th anniversary of Arbor Day (Senator Kenneth Wherry, sponsor)	Nebraska	Burr Oak	*Quercus macrocarpa.*
27	June 26, 1948	Good Templars Tree (plaque placed on existing tree)		American Elm	*Ulmus americana.*
14	April 16, 1949	Memorial to Senator Thomas P. Gore	Oklahoma	Chestnut Oak	*Quercus prinus.*
49	April 16, 1949	Memorial to Senator Robert L. Owen	Oklahoma	Sweet Gum	*Liquidamber styraciflua.*
35	Oct. 11, 1949	Speaker Sam Rayburn	Texas	White Oak	*Quercus alba.*
32	Sept. 2, 1950	Memorial to Representative Chester C. Bolton	Ohio	Buckeye	*Aesculus glabra.*
11	Nov. 16, 1951	Greater North Dakota Association	North Dakota	American Elm	*Ulmus americana.*

Key No.	Date planted	Planted by or memorializing	State	Common name of tree	Botanical name of tree
16	June 12, 1952	Memorial to 5 Sullivan Brothers killed in World War II	Iowa	5 Crab Apples	*Pyrus malus.*
5	April 28, 1954	Senator Leverett Saltonstall	Massachusetts	Red Maple	*Acer rubrum.*
25	July 8, 1954	Speaker Joseph W. Martin, Jr.	Massachusetts	English Elm	*Ulmus procera.*
26	May 17, 1955	Michigan State Society	Michigan	White Pine	*Pinus strobus.*
1	Nov. 13, 1963	State of Georgia (Senator Richard B. Russell, sponsor)	Georgia	Loblolly Pine	*Pinus taeda.*
29	Nov. 18, 1963	Representative Carl Vinson	Georgia	White Oak	*Quercus alba.*
21	Nov. 18, 1963	Representative James C. Auchincloss	New Jersey	Red Oak	*Quercus borealis.*
45	May 13, 1964	Boys' Clubs of America	All States	Red Pine	*Pinus resinosa.*
36	June 11, 1964	Speaker John W. McCormack	Massachusetts	Sugar Maple	*Acer saccharum.*
23	June 11, 1964	Representative Charles A. Halleck	Indiana	Yellow poplar	*Liriodendron tulipifera.*
43	March 17, 1965	Potomac Area Council of Camp Fire Girls (commemorating Founders Day)	District of Columbia	Saucer Magnolia	*Magnolia soulangeania.*
3	April 6, 1965	State Society of New Jersey (Senator Clifford P. Case, sponsor)	New Jersey	Northern Red Oak	*Quercus borealis.*
47	May 3, 1965	Senator Jack Miller	Iowa	Black Walnut	*Juglans nigra.*
46	May 20, 1965	Memorial to Senator Robert S. Kerr	Oklahoma	Redbud	*Cercis canadensis.*
	May 26, 1965	State of New Jersey (Senator Harrison A. Williams, Jr., sponsor)	New Jersey	Red Oak	*Quercus borealis.*
7	March 29, 1966	Congressional Women's Club (Senators' Wives)		Deodar Cedar	*Cedrus deodara.*
31	March 29, 1966	Congressional Women's Club (Representatives' Wives)		Deodar Cedar	*Cedrus deodara.*
48	May 25, 1966	Cherokee Indian Nation (commemorating 200th anniversary of birth of Sequoyah)	Georgia	Redwood	*Sequoia gigantea.*
22	April 3, 1967	State of Ohio (Representative Clarence E. Miller, sponsor)	Ohio	Buckeye	*Aesculus glabra.*
10	April 16, 1967	Arbor Lodge Association of Nebraska City, Nebr. (Senator Carl T. Curtis, sponsor)	Nebraska	Maidenhair	*Ginkgo biloba.*
37	April 28, 1967	Washington Township of New Jersey (Representative John E. Hunt, sponsor)	New Jersey	Cherry Tree	*Prunus Mount Fuji.*
**	May 4, 1967	Mrs. Lyndon B. Johnson		Redbud	*Cercis canadensis.*
12	April 30, 1968	Mrs. Lyndon B. Johnson (Senate Wives, sponsors)		Chinese Dogwood	*Cornus kousa.*
24	May 1, 1969	In Commemoration of the Centennial of Blair, Nebr. (Representative Glenn Cunningham, sponsor)	Nebraska	Blair Maple	*Acer saccarinum Blairi.*
9	June 4, 1969	State of Illinois (dedicated to and planted by Senator Everett M. Dirksen)	Illinois	Pin Oak	*Quercus palustris.*
52	April 14, 1970	State of Tennessee (Representative Richard H. Fulton)	Tennessee	Tulip Poplar	*Liriodendron tulipifera.*
50	Oct. 25, 1971	The Jewish Campaign for the People's Peace Treaty		Bradford Callery Pear	*Pyrus Calleryana Bradford.*

* Memorial or historic tree which has been removed from the Capitol Grounds.
** Memorial or historic tree located in the courtyard of the Everett McKinley Dirksen Office Building.
*** Memorial or historic trees located in the lower West Court Terrace of the Rayburn House Office Building.

Key No.	Date planted	Planted by or memorializing	State	Common name of tree	Botanical name of tree
51	April 28, 1972	Commemoration of the 100th Anniversary of the First Arbor Day Observance		Japanese Zelkova	Zelkova serrata.
54	April 2, 1973	State of Wisconsin (Senator Gaylord Nelson)	Wisconsin	Sugar Maple	Acer saccharum.
53	April 10, 1973	The Senate Ladies Gift to Mrs. Richard M. Nixon		Southern Magnolia	Magnolia grandiflora.
55	Sept. 26, 1974	In Honor of his Retirement, Representative Dave Martin	Nebraska	American Elm	Ulmus americana.
56	Nov. 22, 1974	In Honor of his Retirement, Senator Sam J. Ervin. Jr	North Carolina	White Dogwood	Cornus florida.
57	Dec. 19, 1974	State of Washington (Senator Henry M. Jackson)	Washington	Douglas Fir	Pseudotsuga taxifolia.
58	June 10, 1975	Idaho Federation of Women's Clubs (planted by Senator James A. McClure)	Idaho	White Pine	Pinus strobus.
59	March 12, 1976	In Commemoration of birthdate of Juliet Gordon Lowe (Girl Scout Council of the Nation Capitol Area)		Sassafras	Sassafras albidum.
60	April 5, 1976	State of Maryland (Senator J. Glenn Beall, Jr.)	Maryland	Wye Oak seedling	Quercus alba var. wye.
61	April 27, 1976	In Honor of his Retirement, Senator Roman L. Hruska	Nebraska	Bradford Pear	Pyrus Calleryana Bradford.
62	April 29, 1976	Michigan State Society (Senator Philip A. Hart)	Michigan	American Spruce, Red, White & Blue	Picea Hybrid.
63	May 5, 1976	American Mothers Committee, Inc., Honoring Mothers of America		Crapemyrtle	Lagerstroemia indica.
64	May 6, 1976	Arbor Day Delegation from Nebraska	Nebraska	Cottonwood	Populus deltoides.
65	July 7, 1976	Tulare County American Revolution Bi-Centennial Commission (Plano 4-H Bi-Centennial Flag Corp and Porterville High School Choir)	California	Redwood	Sequoia gigantea.
66	Nov. 22, 1976	Citizens of Paw Paw, West Virginia	West Virginia	Paw Paw	Asimina triloba.
67	Dec. 9, 1976	In Honor of his Retirement, Speaker Carl Albert		Redbud	Cercis canadensis.
68	April 29, 1977	National Arbor Day (Representative Hamilton Fish, Senator Jacob K. Javits and Representative Frederick W. Richmond)		Hybrid Elm	Ulmus Sapporo Autumn Gold.
69	June 6, 1977	1977 Graduation Class (House of Representatives Page School)		Mountain Ash	Sorbus aucuparia.
70	March 15, 1978	Members of the Texas Delegation, 95th Congress	Texas	Hybrid Pecan	Carya ill. var. Kiowa.
71	March 27, 1978	Liberty Tree seedling (Senator Charles McC. Mathias)	Maryland	Tulip Poplar	Liriodendron tulipifera.
***	May 25, 1978	Republican Congressional Wives Honoring Mrs. Richard Nixon and Mrs. Gerald Ford (Mrs. Gerald Ford)		Golden-chain	Laburnum anagyroides.
72	June 12, 1978	1978 Graduation Class (House of Representatives Page School)		Mountain Ash	Sorbus aucuparia.
73	Oct. 5, 1978	California State Society (Representative Fortney H. Stark, Jr.)	California	Redwood	Sequoia gigantea.
74	March 23, 1979	In Honor of his Retirement, Representative Olin E. Teague		Bradford Pear	Pyrus Calleryana Bradford.
75	June 11, 1979	1979 Graduation Class (House of Representatives Page School)		Japanese Pagoda	Sophora Japonica.

Botanic Gardens

The United States Botanic Garden was founded in 1820 under the auspices of the Columbia Institute for the Promotion of Arts and Sciences, an outgrowth of an association known as the Metropolitan Society, which received its charter from Congress on April 20, 1818. The Botanic Garden continued under the direction of this Institute until 1837, when the Institute ceased to exist as an active organization.

The Botanic Garden thereafter remained abandoned until 1842, when it became necessary for the Government to provide accommodations for the botanical collections brought to Washington, D.C. from the South Seas by the U.S. Exploring Expedition of 1838–1842, under the leadership of Captain Charles Wilkes. The collection was temporarily placed on exhibition on a lot behind the Patent Office building. A greenhouse was constructed under the direction and control of Congress' Joint Committee on the Library. Upon completion of the greenhouse, the collection from the exploring expedition was placed therein and was put under the custodianship of the Commissioner of Patents by the Library Committee. The actual care of the botanical collections was under the supervision of Captain Wilkes, assisted by William D. Brackenridge, a horticulturist and assistant botanist for the expedition.

In 1849 Congress authorized the construction of an extension to the Patent Office building, making it necessary to relocate the Botanic Garden greenhouses annexed thereto. The site selected by the Joint Committee on the Library for the relocation was at the west end of the Capitol Grounds, practically the same location as that occupied by the Botanic Garden during the period it functioned under the Columbia Institute. The construction of a new greenhouse on this site was placed under the supervision of

United States Botanic Garden

the Architect of the Capitol, with the approval of the Joint Committee on the Library.

For many years following this relocation, there existed an intention to secure for the Botanic Garden more adequate facilities for carrying on its work, to place it on a level with other botanic gardens throughout the country.

On January 7, 1925, Congress took definite steps toward this goal by authorizing the preparation of preliminary plans, and later approved the project by authorization of funds for the site, for the construction of new conservatories and other necessary buildings and for the relocation of the Bartholdi fountain.

The Bartholdi fountain was originally exhibited at the 1876 International Exhibition held in Philadelphia, and had been purchased by the U.S. Government in 1877 for six thousand dollars. The architect of the fountain was Frederic Auguste Bartholdi, a French sculptor who also designed the Statue of Liberty.

The fountain is constructed of bronzed iron, cast in Paris by A. Dureene. The entire structure is thirty feet high, and rests in the center of a large marble basin, supported by a triangular pedestal, on the faces of which are aquatic reptiles and fishes spouting water. Upon this pedestal stand three female caryatids supporting another basin, from the rim of which twelve Victorian lamps are suspended gracefully. The fountain is surmounted by a crown, through which the water flows.

Interior of Botanic Garden.

Bartholdi Fountain

Interior of Botanic Garden.

Interior of Botanic Garden

The cornerstone of the new conservatory was laid on November 12, 1931; the new buildings were occupied on January 13, 1933.

Structurally, the design of the new conservatory follows conventional form, with an arched and domed roof frame carrying the great expanse of glass sheathing. In its details the design presents many points of interest, among which is the extensive use of aluminum for structural members—the first time aluminum had been used for such purposes. The main feature is the one-story loggia or entrance hall forming the Maryland Avenue front. It is built of limestone, carried to a height of about 40 feet and has a series of lofty arched doorways. The main conservatory is approximately 262 feet in length and 183 feet in width.

The square across Independence Avenue south of the Conservatory was developed as an outdoor garden—this is the site of the relocated Bartholdi fountain. The Botanic Garden property also includes more than 22 acres known as Poplar Point Nursery, adjacent to Anacostia Park. This property was added to the United States Botanic Garden in 1926.

Summer at the Botanic Garden.

Perennials in bloom

Outdoor garden located across Independence Avenue south of conservatory

Art in the Capitol

The Capitol itself can be considered a work of art. The classical architecture and the interior embellishments from Latrobe's corn cob capitals to Brumidi's powerful dome painting provide this beautiful ambience. A complete survey of the various paintings, sculptures, and decorative details found in the Capitol is available in the catalog, Art in the U.S. Capitol (House Document 94–660), prepared by the Architect of the Capitol under the direction of the Joint Committee on the Library.

The following pages provide only a few examples of the artistic treasures found in the Capitol.

Brumidi's dome and frieze paintings complement the classical cast iron details of Thomas Walter's dome. Vinnie Ream's statue of Abraham Lincoln stands in the foreground.

Thomas Jefferson and Benjamin Latrobe designed the corn cob capitals for the columns in the foyer outside the Old Supreme Court Chamber (1809).

Some of Brumidi's most beautiful room paintings are found in S–127, the Senate Committee on Appropriations room. Pompeian architecture and allegorical figures dominate the compositions on all the walls and ceiling.

On the first floor of the Senate corridor Brumidi painted walls and ceilings with medallion portraits, sketches of major inventions, and paintings of birds, animals and flowers.

The ceiling in the Presidents Room is ornately decorated. This allegoric female figure is reminiscent of earlier Italian paintings of Madonnas.

The President's Room,
with frescoes and oil
paintings, dates to about
1860. Until the 1930s
Presidents signed bills at
the mahogany table under
the great crystal
chandelier.

Drawn by Thomas U. Walter this study shows the skeletal arrangement of the dome's interior ironwork.

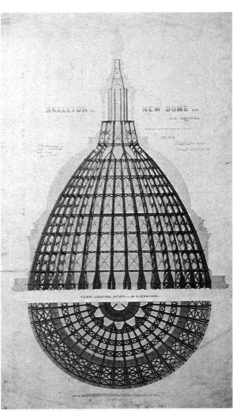

"Washington at Valley Forge, 1778" is on the south wall of the Senate Appropriations room.

"Calling of Putnam From the Plow to the Revolution" is on the west wall of the House Appropriations room. Putnam left his farm to fight in the Battle of Breed's Hill, June 16, 1775.

"Scene at the Signing of the Constitution", by Howard Chandler Christy, was commissioned by Congress in 1940 for the east stairway of the House Wing. This 20 x 30 foot canvas, largest in the Capitol, is remarkable for its historic detail and its patriotic inspiration. Eleven years after independence was declared, the leaders of the new nation met in Independence Hall, Sept. 17, 1787 to place their names on this modern document of freedom. Well known likenesses of George Washington, Benjamin Franklin, Alexander Hamilton, James Madison, are easily recognized.

"First Reading of the Emancipation Proclamation", by Francis B. Carpenter, in west staircase of Senate Wing. Lincoln is shown with his cabinet. Seated; Edwin M. Stanton, President Lincoln, Gideon Welles, William H. Seward, Edward Bates; standing; Salmon P. Chase, Caleb B. Smith, Montgomery Blair.

"George Washington" by Rembrandt Peale. This distinguished portrait is known because of its illusionistically painted frame as the "porthole portrait." Purchased for the Senate in 1832 it hangs in the Old Senate Chamber.

"The Declaration of Independence", one of the eight paintings in the Rotunda, depicts a monumental event in our history in Independence Hall, Philadelphia, July 4, 1776. The 56 signers, all members of the Continental Congress, risked death to tell the world that "for the support of this Declaration . . . we mutually pledge to each other our Lives, our Fortunes, and our sacred Honor".

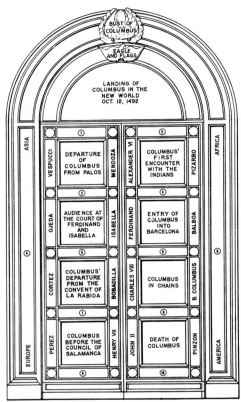

Diagram of bronze doors
of the main entrance to
Rotunda—East Front
United States Capitol

Within the diagram:

BUST OF COLUMBUS

EAGLE AND FLAGS

LANDING OF
COLUMBUS IN THE
NEW WORLD
OCT. 12, 1492

ASIA

VESPUCCI — ① DEPARTURE OF COLUMBUS FROM PALOS — MENDOZA

ALEXANDER VI — ③ COLUMBUS' FIRST ENCOUNTER WITH THE INDIANS — PIZARRO

AFRICA

OJEDA — ③ AUDIENCE AT THE COURT OF FERDINAND AND ISABELLA — ISABELLA

FERDINAND — ④ ENTRY OF COLUMBUS INTO BARCELONA — BALBOA

CORTEZ — ⑤ COLUMBUS' DEPARTURE FROM THE CONVENT OF LA RABIDA — BOBADILLA

CHARLES VIII — ⑥ COLUMBUS IN CHAINS — B. COLUMBUS

EUROPE

PEREZ — ⑦ COLUMBUS BEFORE THE COUNCIL OF SALAMANCA — HENRY VII

JOHN II — ⑧ DEATH OF COLUMBUS — PINZON

AMERICA

The Columbus Doors,
designed by Randolph
Rogers, originally hung in
the corridor connecting
Statuary Hall with the
House Wing. In 1871 they
were moved to the East
Front entrance.

Inside the Capitol dome. Constantino Brumidi's "Apotheosis of Washington", the fresco in the canopy of the dome, is a masterful allegorical work of art. Brumidi worked 11 months painting this masterpiece; he signed it in 1865. The 13 original colonies surround Washington, who is flanked by Liberty and Victory and Fame. Other allegorical figures averaging 25 feet in height symbolize the Arts and Sciences, the Sea, Commerce, Mechanics, Agriculture, War and Freedom.

"C. Brumidi Artist, Citizen of the U.S." is how Brumidi signed "Cornwallis Sues for Cessation of Hostilities Under the Flag of Truce". The fresco, once in the House of Representatives is now in the House Dining Room.

Gods and mortals mingle in the Dome's fresco. (1) Ceres rides a reaper as Young America, wearing a liberty cap, stands near. (2) Vulcan rests his foot on a cannon. (3) Bearded Neptune and Aphrodite, holding the Atlantic cable, rise from the sea. (4) Sandaled Mercury offers a bag of gold to Robert Morris, "Financier of the Revolution." (5) Wise Minerva speaks to Benjamin Franklin, S. F. B. Morse, and Robert Fulton. (6) Armed Freedom—Brumidi's young wife was the model—triumphs over Tyranny and Kingly Power.

5

6

Lawgivers Who Advanced the March to Human Freedom

*The Law of Old
and of Today
Seek to Glorify
the Dignity of Man*

Location of the 23 Marble
Relief Portraits Over the
Gallery Doors, House of
Representatives

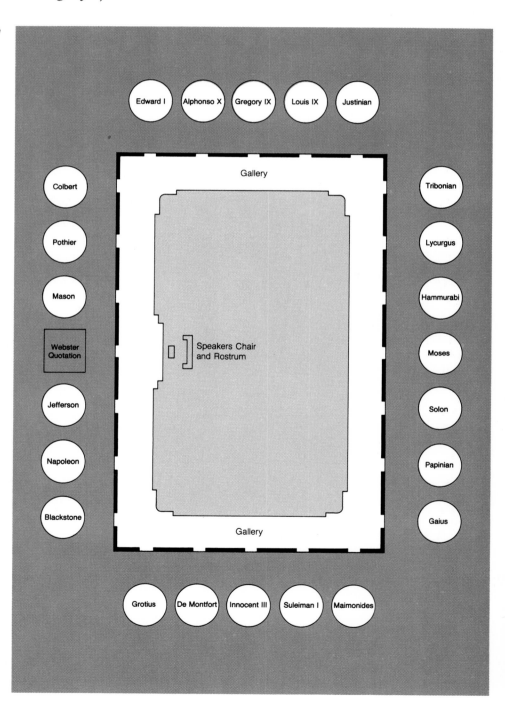

The United States Congress today has awesome, world-wide responsibilities. One of its little-reflected-upon tasks, however, is one of its most important. The Congress today must pick up the mantle of a centuries-old struggle: to develop and improve upon a workable, enforceable, and equitable system of justice.

The founding fathers performed a remarkable feat during that long hot Philadephia summer in 1787. They did not, however, start from scratch. They drew upon the knowledge and wisdom, and the failures, of three thousand years of recorded history. Any visitor to the House Chamber will appreciate the fact that our modern law-makers are building upon a priceless heritage of Western civilization.

As a constant reminder of its task, the Congress directed that the upper walls of the House Chamber be adorned with 23 marble relief portraits of noted "Lawgivers". Created in bas relief on white Vermont marble, by seven different sculptors, the plaques each measure 28" in diameter. One is full face; the other 22 are profiles. From the full face of Moses on the north wall, 11 profiles face left and 11 face right, ending at a quotation from Daniel Webster on the south wall above the Speaker's chair.

The subjects of the plaques were jointly chosen by a group from the University of Pennsylvania and the Columbia Historical Society of Washington, D.C., in consultation with expert staff from the Library of Congress. The selection was approved by a special committee of five Members of the House of Representatives, the Architect of the Capitol, and his associates.

The struggle for an effective and equitable system of justice has been slow and uncertain. The world has suffered far more often under the yoke of despots than it has prospered under a rule of law. In fact, even in the histories of some of the celebrated lawgivers displayed in the House Chamber, lives of despotism and ruthlessness mix with noble resolve and high motive. However, taken in the context of their times, their individual contributions served to advance the rule of law. As a free people, we do right to honor their contributions.

Hammurabi

The Babylonian king and lawgiver. More than seventeen hundred years before Christ—according to the latest chronology—he gave to his age and to mankind, the code of laws that bears his name. Historically one of the first four lawgivers known to civilization, he ruled his people justly—"that the strong shall not oppress the weak"— and through law gave his people contentment and prosperity.

Moses

The Hebrew lawgiver and prophet, thundered the Ten Commandments from Mount Sinai more than three thousand years ago. He was the great administrator who created a nation, cementing law with religion, and giving to the ages a tough moral code that is the foundation for the noblest ideas of man on the dignity of the individual.

Lycurgus

Lawgiver of Sparta who reformed its constitution about the seventh or ninth century B.C. He established a more equitable basis for the ownership of property and is said to have enacted laws so sound they remained in force nearly a thousand years.

Solon

Athenian statesman, businessman and legislator, known as one of the Seven Wise Men of Greece, who about 595 B.C. may be said to have pioneered a form of democratic government by cutting down the unlimited powers of the nobility. Citizens were granted juries to act as courts of last instance. Under the great new law code he erected, contracts were illegal that bartered a man's liberty.

Gaius

Roman jurist whose most important work, *Institutes,* a popular manual of Roman law, was incorporated almost bodily in the widely known *Institutes of Justinian.* He flourished around the second century of the Christian era, giving us what many believe is the first elementary textbook on the law in the modern sense.

Papinian

About 200 A.D., a strict moralist, is regarded among the greatest of the Roman jurists.

Justinian

Roman Emperor, 483–565 A.D., made his contribution as a legislator and a jurist, giving the world the Code of Justinian, compiled by a commission of lawyers he appointed. This *Corpus Juris Civilis* is said to constitute the nucleus of nearly all modern European systems, and to have influenced the common law of England.

Tribonian

Died 545, was Justinian's top law officer. Law editor and Director of the compilation of Justinian's *Corpus Juris Civilis,* he gave to posterity the benefit of his vast technical knowledge of Roman Law.

Maimonides

1135–1204, rabbi, physician, law-codifier, profoundly influenced non-Jewish as well as Jewish thought, with his monumental work organizing and systematizing Jewish oral law. Widely known also is his *Guide For The Perplexed* which has been translated into English.

Gregory IX

Pope, 1145–1241, promulgated an impressive compilation of decretals—a collection of decrees—as a standard textbook in canon law.

Innocent III

Pope, 1161–1216, active and diligent as a judge, respected for his judicial impartiality, stands as one of the foremost figures of medieval times.

de Montfort

Died 1265, championed the cause of the nobles and the people against the king—thereby establishing a precedent—and created a place for himself in history by calling the Great Parliament which brought together for this assembly representatives from towns and boroughs.

Louis IX

1214–70, King of France, canonized in 1297. His rule was marked by justice and competence and he has been characterized as the ideal king of the Middle Ages.

Alfonzo X

1221–84, Spanish King and patron of learning, is credited with doing much for the *Siete Partidas,* a compilation of Roman and canon law.

Edward I

1239–1307, King of England, sometimes called the English Justinian. He compiled the Statutes of Westminster, influenced striking developments in law and espoused constitutional principles.

Suleiman I

1494–1566, Sultan of the Turkish Empire. Distinguished in Turkish history as The Lawyer and in European history as The Magnificent, he improved the status of Christians in his domains, and set up a new and better system of laws to govern an empire he widely extended. He won himself immortality as a legislator.

Grotius

1583–1645, Dutch jurist and humanist. His *De jure belli et pacis* has been called "one of the greatest masterpieces of legal literature". This work is remarkable for its originality and its thinking on international law and international ethics.

Colbert

1619–83, French statesman, who improved the administration of justice, codified the ordinances and reformed the French legal system.

Pothier

1699–1772, French jurist. A scholar of Roman and French law, his monographs on the laws of his country were in many instances incorporated in the French Civil Code. His work on the Roman law revealed profound scholarship.

Blackstone

1723–80, English jurist. His *Commentaries on the Laws of England* constitute a standard textbook on the subject, and his fame is perhaps even greater in the United States than in his native land.

Mason

1725–92, American statesman. He succeeded Washington in the Virginia convention and drafted the Bill of Rights, basic to the Constitution of the United States, as well as the Constitutions of many of the States of the Union. Mason's influence extended to the French Declaration of the Rights of Man.

Bonaparte

1769–1821, Emperor of France. He directed the codification of French law, the *Code Napoleon,* which is the basis for the law of France, and has been adopted in many parts of Europe. Actually the work of the most eminent lawyers of France of that time, it combined old French laws with laws envisaging the new revolutionary legal philosophy of France and with laws conceived by Napoleon himself.

Jefferson

1743–1826, third President of the United States, author of the Declaration of Independence and of the statute of religious freedom in the constitution of Virginia. He is among a small handful of American statesmen who have exerted a major and continuing influence on the basic institutions of the United States, and on the free world, and who is a foremost American immortal in world history.

Architects of the Capitol

Responsibilities of the Architect of the Capitol

Senator Claiborne Pell of Rhode Island, Chairman, Senate Rules and Administration Committee (left) meets with William McWhorter Cochrane, Committee Staff Director (right) and George C. White, Architect of the Capitol (center) prior to hearing.

The incumbent Architect of the Capitol, George M. White, FAIA, is the ninth holder of this office, first occupied by Dr. William Thornton, who was appointed by President Washington in 1793 after his design for the permanent Capitol Building in the new Federal capital district was selected winner in a national architectural competition. Dr. Thornton's responsibilities were limited to design and supervision of construction of the new Capitol Building, under direction of the Commissioners of the Federal District and the President of the United States.

The role and responsibilities of the Architect have changed and grown as increased activities have been assigned to the office by the Congress.

The Architect of the Capitol is still charged with the planning, design and construction of such buildings as may be committed to his care by Congress from time to time. Current projects include construction of the Library of Congress James Madison Memorial Building; expansion, modification and enlargement of the facilities of the Capitol Power Plant; construction and equipment of an extension to the Dirksen Office Building; acquisition of additional property as part of the Capitol Grounds; and extension, reconstruction, alteration and improvement of the additional House Office Building projects.

Permanent authority for the care and maintenance of the Capitol Building is provided by the act of August 15, 1876 (19 Stat. 147; 40 U.S.C. 162–163). Appropriate legislation has been enacted from time to time to provide for the care and maintenance of the additional buildings and grounds placed under the jurisdiction of the Architect of the Capitol by Congress over the years.

Although appointment to the office is made by the President, the Architect then becomes a part of the Legislative Branch and serves as an officer and agent of the Congress.

The Architect is charged with the direction and supervision, as well as

with the structural and mechanical care, of all improvements, alterations, additions and repairs to the following buildings and grounds, including operation of the mechanical equipment:

Capitol Building (including domestic care of the building except for the Senate wing)
Capitol Grounds
Senate Office Buildings (including domestic care)
House Office Buildings (including domestic care)
Library of Congress Buildings and Grounds
United States Supreme Court Building and Grounds
Capitol Power Plant
Senate Garage
Robert A. Taft Memorial

The Architect performs his duties in connection with the Senate side of the Capitol, the Senate Office Buildings and the Senate Garage, subject to the approval of the Senate Committee on Rules and Administration as to matters of general policy; in connection with the House Office Buildings and the Capitol Power Plant, his activities are subject to approval and direction of the House Office Building Commission; and he is under the direction of the Speaker in matters concerning the House side of the Capitol.

The Architect is also charged with the operation of the:

United States Botanic Garden (as Acting Director, under the direction of the Joint Committee on the Library)
Senate Restaurants (under the direction of the Senate Committee on Rules and Administration)

William Thornton

Early schooling in Lancashire, England. Spent 3 years at University of Edinburgh studying medicine. Was graduated in 1784 with M.D. from Aberdeen University. Co-experimented with John Fitch in designing a steamboat. Self-taught architect and portrait painter. Won the competition for designing the United States Capitol in 1793. As Architect, supervised the beginning construction of the original North or Senate wing. Appointed as one of three District Commissioners, he continued supervising construction of the Capitol. Superintendents during this period were Stephen Hallet, James Hoban and George Hadfield.

William Thornton

Born May 20, 1759, Jost van Dyke, West Indies
Died March 28, 1828, Washington, D.C.
Appointed by President George Washington, 1793
Resigned September 12, 1794

Benjamin Henry Latrobe

Classic education at Fulneck School, Yorkshire, England. Entered college at Niesky and tradition says he also studied 3 years at University of Leipzig. Studied engineering with John Smeaton and entered the office of S. P. Cockerell, architect. Fellow of the American Philosophical Society; member of American Antiquarian Society and Philadelphia Academy of Arts; vice president of Society of Artists of the United States; honorary member of Academy of Arts; member of Chemical Society of Philadelphia. Constructed the original House wing and remodeled the interior of the original Senate wing; after the fire of 1814 he redesigned and constructed the interiors of both wings, now Statuary Hall and the Old Senate Chamber.

Benjamin Henry Latrobe

Born May 1, 1764, England
Died September 3, 1820, New Orleans, Louisiana
Appointed by President Thomas Jefferson March 6, 1803—resigned July 1, 1811
Appointed by President James Madison April 6, 1815—resigned November 20, 1817

Charles Bulfinch

Classic education at Latin School, was graduated from Harvard in 1781. Studied architecture in Europe and devoted himself seriously to the study of architecture to become New England's leading architect. Member of the National Academy of Design. One of the first American born architects of distinction. Constructed the center section and the original low wooden dome of the Capitol. His design also extended the West Front from that planned by Latrobe. He planned the landscaping and the original earthen west terraces. From

Charles Bulfinch

Born August 8, 1763, Boston, Mass.
Died April 15, 1844, Boston, Mass.
Appointed by President James Monroe January 8, 1818
Office abolished June 25, 1829

1829 to 1851

From 1829 to 1851 there was no Architect of the Capitol because the office had been abolished. Necessary services were performed by the Commissioner of Public Buildings and Grounds until 1836 when the Architect of Public Buildings, Robert Mills, was put in charge of maintenance. He was never Architect of the Capitol.

Thomas Ustick Walter

Apprenticed as a young boy to his father who was a bricklayer and mason. Strong education in mathematical studies, physical sciences, cultivation of the arts of drawing and painting, and practical knowledge of mechanical construction. Student of architecture and mechanical drawing in the office of William Strickland. Became a practicing architect in 1830. Sent to Europe by the Building Committee of Girard College to study building improvements in general. One of the founders of the American Institute of Architects and its second president; member of Franklin Institute of Pennsylvania and American Philosophical Society; honorary M.A. from Madison University in New York, 1849; Ph. D. from University of Lewisburg, Pennsylvania in 1853; and LL.D. from Harvard, 1857. Won the competition for the design to extend the wings of the Capitol and executed this work; was architect for the present high, iron dome; reconstructed interior of west center building to provide for the Library of Congress after the fire of 1851. Made first studies for extending the East and West Central Fronts of the Capitol.

Thomas Ustick Walter

Born Sept. 4, 1804,
Philadelphia, Pa.
Died Oct. 30, 1887,
Philadelphia, Pa.
Appointed by President
Millard Fillmore June 11,
1851
Resigned May 26, 1865

Edward Clark

Studied freehand and mechanical drawing under his architect father, James Clark. Received special training in engineering from his uncle, Thomas Clark, an Army engineer. Student of Thomas U. Walter, and under him was made superintendent of construction on the Patent Office and Post Office in 1857 and assistant to Walter in adding the wings and dome to the Capitol. Fellow in American Institute of Architects and well known in many scientific, literary and musical societies. Oversaw completion of the porticoes of the new wings; reconstructed the Old Hall of Representatives for use as Statuary Hall; extended Capitol Grounds and built present granite terraces; reconstructed and repaired Old Supreme Court section after explosion and fire of 1898; replaced gas with electricity; reconstructed West central floors vacated by Library of Congress when it moved to its present building in 1897; supervised installation of elevators, fireproofing, incandescent lights, modernized heating and ventilating.

Edward Clark

Born August 15, 1822,
Philadelphia, Pennsylvania
Died January 6, 1902,
Washington, D.C.
Appointed by President
Andrew Johnson August
30, 1865
Died in office January 6,
1902

Elliott Woods

Educated in Indianapolis, Indiana. Associated with Architect's office 17 years prior to his appointment as Architect. Also served as architect or associate architect in the erection of public buildings in Washington, D.C. Deeply interested in scientific pursuits, he became known for his work in X-ray and radio and telegraphy. Member of American Institute of Architects. Oversaw the erection of the first House and Senate Office Buildings and subways; built the Capitol Power Plant; added 5th floor to Cannon House Office Building; built 28 rooms in the space formerly occupied by the Library of Congress in the Capitol; made significant changes in lighting, heating and ventilating.

Elliott Woods

Born February 2, 1865
near Manchester, England
Died May 22, 1923, Spring
Lake, New Jersey
Appointed by President
Theodore Roosevelt
February 19, 1902
Died in office May 22,
1923

David Lynn

Educated in public schools of Cumberland, Maryland and the Allegheny County Academy. Entered the Office of the Architect under Edward Clark and became 7th Architect of the Capitol 21 years later upon the death of Elliott Woods. Honorary member of American Institute of Architects. Responsible for construction of the Longworth House Office Building; U.S. Supreme Court Building; Library of Congress Annex; First Street wing of the Old Senate Office Building; built the Senate Garage and expanded the Capitol Grounds; added to the powerplant; remodeled the Senate and House Chambers; constructed the Botanic Garden Conservatory; and began construction of the New Senate Office Building.

David Lynn

Born November 10, 1873,
Wheeling, West Virginia
Died May 25, 1961,
Washington, D.C.
Appointed by President
Calvin Coolidge August
22, 1923
Retired September 30,
1954

J. George Stewart

Early schooling in Wilmington; engineering degree from University of Delaware; licensed professional engineer, State of Delaware; president of his own general construction firm; Representative in Congress, 1935–37; Clerk of the District of Columbia Committee, U.S. Senate; engineer consultant to Lands Division, Department of Justice, and Corps of Engineers. Honorary member of American Institute of Architects, honorary fellow American Registered Architects. Continued the work of his predecessor in construction of New Senate Office Building and connecting subways; continued improvements and expansion of the powerplant; approved plans for Taft Memorial and bell tower; prepared the Prayer Room for Congressional use; extended East Central Front of the Capitol and rehabilitated the Dome; responsible for construction of Rayburn House Office Building, connecting subway and the House underground garages; remodeled Cannon House Office Building and prepared plans for full remodeling of Longworth House Office Building; initiated improved interior and exterior lighting of the Capitol; responsible for preliminary plans for the James Madison Memorial Library of Congress Building and extension of the West Central Front of the Capitol.

J. George Stewart

Born June 2, 1890,
Wilmington, Delaware
Died May 24, 1970,
Washington, D.C.
Appointed by President
Dwight D. Eisenhower
October 1, 1954
Died in office May 24,1970

George Malcolm White

Graduate of Massachusetts Institute of Technology with a B.S. and M.S. in Electrical Engineering; M.B.A. Harvard; J.D., Case Western Reserve; Registered Architect in Ohio and District of Columbia; Registered Engineer in Ohio, Massachusetts and District of Columbia; member of Bar of Ohio and District of Columbia; and the Supreme Court of the United States; certified by the National Council of Architectural Registration Boards and National Council of Engineering Examiners. A former electronics design engineer; has practiced as an architect and consulting engineer since 1948 and as a lawyer since 1960; former member of the faculty at Case Western Reserve in physics and architecture; Fellow of American Institute of Architects and former Vice President; member of National Panel of Arbitrators of the American Arbitration Association; member of National Society of Professional Engineers; member of American Bar Association; and Gold Medalist of Architects Society of Ohio. Ex-officio, a member of the Zoning Commission of the District of Columbia, the U.S. Capitol Police Board, and a Director of the Pennsylvania Avenue Development Corporation. Acting Director of the U.S. Botanic Garden. Responsible for construction of the James Madison Memorial Library of Congress Building; restoration of Old Supreme Court and Old Senate Chambers in the Capitol; design of the extension to the Dirksen Office Building; expansion program for the Capitol Power Plant; space studies of Senate and House facilities; master planning efforts for Capitol Hill; alterations to buildings on Capitol Hill to provide barrier-free design for the handicapped; modification of two passageways on House side of Capitol; revisions to interior of Supreme Court building.

George Malcolm White

Born November 1, 1920,
Cleveland, Ohio
Appointed by President
Richard M. Nixon
January 27, 1971

Visitors and Guide Service

The Capitol
Guide Service.

Enthralled visitors

There are many works of
art in the Rotunda to
interest visitors.

The people who visit the Capitol of the United States come for many reasons and from a multitude of backgrounds. The Nation's citizens visit the Capitol with feelings of ownership, pride and unity; they come to see the place where the President is inaugurated, to see the workings of their government, to meet their representatives, to show their children the National heritage. And from around the world, millions come each year to see one of the greatest living symbols of freedom and self-government.

Before these visitors, the Capitol spreads a story, depicted alike in paintings, sculpture, architecture and daily business—the struggle of a people to govern themselves, to be and to remain free.

It is vital to our form of Government that the people be able to see and hear the machinery of legislation in motion. In the House and Senate Chambers, visitors watch from galleries while the Members of Congress debate the issues of Government.

The people also speak. Many come to seek counsel with their Representatives or Senators. They may need help, or wish to make known their position on matters of legislation.

Perhaps the most important visitors are the students, the young people of the world who visit the Capitol and see its workings, its spirit and its substance. Many have studied the forms and history of U.S. Government, but without these visits they can have little idea of the vast range of activities behind the final acts of legislation.

It is an "open" Capitol. Visitors roam the halls and grounds of the Capitol Hill complex at their leisure. Tours and signs and guidebooks are offered to increase the value of their visiting time.

Groups of individuals may request admittance to the House and Senate galleries from their Representative or Senator. The Member writes a letter to the proper official, requesting that the

This "Head of Lincoln" by Gutzon Borglum was a model for the artist's work at Mt. Rushmore.

This view of the small Senate Rotunda show the Latrobe tobacco leaf capitals and a later nineteenth century chandelier.

This replica of Magna Carta was presented to the Capitol during the Bicentennial celebration.

One of the stops on the tour is a Brumidi corridor.

The size of the Rotunda painting and sculpted reliefs reminds the viewer of the giant scale of this area.

group be admitted, with a copy of the letter to the group leader, who shows it to the Doorkeeper.

Individuals may also obtain passes for admission to the House Gallery from a Representative; admission to the Senate Gallery is gained by a pass issued by a Senator. The two passes are not interchangeable, and they do not admit the bearer to special events or to the Joint Session of the Congress. House Gallery passes are good for both sessions of Congress. Senate Gallery passes are good for only one session.

One organization is authorized by Congress to provide tours, at no charge, through the interior of the United States Capitol.

The original Guide Service was established in 1876 as an outgrowth of the Philadelphia Centennial and the resultant increased volume of visitors to the United States Capitol Building. Guides were unsalaried employees appointed by the Congress who derived

their income from the 25 cent fee that was charged for the tour. This system remained in effect until January 3, 1971, when Title IV, Part 4 of Public Law 91–510 ". . . established an organization under the Congress of the United States, to be designated the 'Capitol Guide Service'. . .".

Jurisdiction over the Capitol Guide Service was vested in the Committee on Rules and Administration of the Senate and the Committee on House Administration of the House of Representatives. The Capitol Guide Board, composed of the two Sergeants At Arms and the Architect of the Capitol was created to direct, supervise and control the Capitol Guide Service.

Public tours of the Capitol Building are offered between 9:00 a.m. and 3:45 p.m., seven days a week except for Thanksgiving, Christmas and New Year's Day. Tours begin at least every 15 minutes and during the busy season as frequently as every two minutes. They cover as many points

of interest as possible coincident with existing conditions within the Capitol Building. Over 67 percent of the visitors to the Capitol visit during the five months of April through August of each year.

A Capitol guide leads a tour.

This grand staircase is one of two that serve the House of Representatives.

The center of the Rotunda floor was once open. Closed by Bulfinch this area is now the spot where American heroes lay in state.

Music at the Capitol

Music Maestro, Please

That "music hath charms" is well recognized by the Congress. The Capitol and the House and Senate office buildings resound, especially during the spring and summer months, with all types of music. From the majestic inspiration of the National Symphony, and the stirring marches of the military bands to the tunes of Gershwin and the tones of Roberta Flack, the visitors to the Capitol can enjoy whatever suits their taste.

The American Festival Concerts at the Capitol sponsored by the United States Congress and the Secretary of the Interior which are performed by the National Symphony and under the direction of such maestros as Aaron Copland, Mstislav Rostropovich, Erich Leinsdorf, and the late Arthur Fiedler have delighted hundreds of thousands of music lovers from all over the world. The Service bands, and choral groups, of the Air Force, Army, Marine Corps and Navy provide summer night entertainment for other thousands in concerts that have become a Capitol tradition.

Perhaps more thrilling to the individual musician concerned are the hundreds of performances every spring by the high school and college bands from all over the United States who visit the Nation's Capital and perform at the Capitol. In addition the Capitol and its various office buildings are filled throughout the year but especially during the winter holiday season with the joyous voices of choral groups.

These appearances are arranged well in advance by the Senators or Representatives through the Architect of the Capitol.

Without this music, the Capitol would be a far more sombre place indeed.

A member of the Air Force Band performs at the Capitol. Note the reflection of the Capitol in the instrument.

The President's Own, the Marine Corps Band performing on the West Front of the Capitol.

A member of the Navy Band performing during a summer concert on the Capitol steps.

The National Symphony performs on the West Lawn of the Capitol.

The Air Force Band during an evening concert at the Capitol.

Members of the Air Force Band percussion section performing on the West Front of the Capitol.

The Sea Chanters of the Navy Band perform the Man from La Mancha at the Capitol.

The Navy Band ceremonial unit.

The United States Army Band marching down Pennsylvania Avenue from the Capitol.

The Marine Corps Band at the Capitol.

One of the many high school marching bands to perform at the Capitol.

The Air Force Band performs as hundreds listen on the steps of the West Front of the Capitol.

The Navy Band and Sea Chanters.

A high school band from Sacramento, California performs at the Capitol.

Congress as an Institution

Aerial view of the Capitol, East Front with House Chamber on left and Senate Chamber on right.

Aerial view of the Capitol, West Front

*Official portrait of the
United States
House of Representatives,
September 19, 1979.*

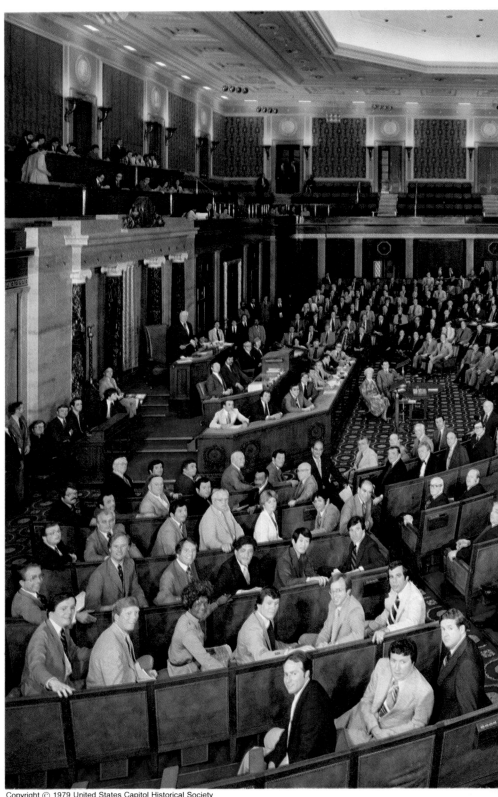

The Congress was created by Article I of the Constitution which vests all legislative powers granted by the people to the Government in the Senate and the House of Representatives. Section 1 of Article I establishes the specific structure and powers of the House of Representatives.

Currently the House is limited to 435 Representatives elected by the voters of the fifty States. In addition, one Delegate each represents the voters of the District of Columbia, Guam and the Virgin Islands. Puerto Rico is represented by the Resident Commissioner. These latter four persons do not vote on the passage of bills, although they do vote in committee to approve a bill to be considered by the total House.

States are assigned the number of Representatives based on the decennial census. Each Member represents approximately 450,000 constituents. Each State is entitled to at least one Representative, even though the population of the State may be less than 450,000. The State legislature defines the geographic boundaries of the Congressional District whose voters elect the Representative every two years. If a Representative dies or leaves office in mid-term the Governor of the State calls a special election to choose a replacement.

Any citizen over the age of 25, who has been a citizen of the United States for at least seven years, may be elected to serve in the House of Representatives, providing that he or she is a resident of the State at the time of election. Senators must be 30 years of age.

Unlike the Senate, whose Members represent the States, the Representatives' powers do not overlap those of the Executive and Judicial branches of the Federal Government. They do not confirm Presidential appointments. The House does not vote on ratification treaties. The House can vote on articles of impeachment, i.e., an indictment of the President or other Federal officer, but the Senate judges whether or not the officer is removed from office.

The major strength of the House lies in its power to initiate "money" bills—taxation and appropriation measures. The Senate may vote changes in such bills, but the differences are resolved in conference between the House and Senate.

Because of the large number of Representatives, the House has of necessity developed more restrictive rules on debate than those which apply to the Senate. The Rules Committee of the House determines the order in which bills come to the floor for action, the time limit during which a bill may be considered, whether or not—and how many—amendments to the bill may be proposed.

As in the Senate, the major activity of the House, especially in the early months of each session, is in the committees, which receive all bills introduced on the subject of a committee's jurisdiction. The committees are divided into subcommittees which conduct hearings, add amendments and either approve or reject the bills. If approved, the bill is considered by the full committee which can reject, amend and approve, or decline to act on the measure. If approved, the bill goes to the Rules Committee for scheduling for floor action.

When a bill is granted a rule, it comes before the House which resolves itself into the Committee of the Whole. In this status the House debates the bill, considers and accepts or rejects amendments. The Committee of the Whole then resolves itself into the House of Representatives and votes on each amendment and lastly on final passage.

The House meets in the House Chamber in the South wing of the Capitol. Members are not assigned specific seats as in the Senate. The Majority party members sit on the right of the Speaker's rostrum. the Minority on the left. As in the Senate Chamber, the press and media galleries are above the Speaker's gallery. The public are seated in the side and rear galleries; seats are available to those who secure passes from their Representatives on a first come, first served basis.

Mace of the House of Representatives. This ensign of authority, topped by the high flying eagle, is also a signal of information to the Members of the House. An assistant Sergeant at Arms sets it at the right of the Speaker when the House is called to order each day. There it remains in position while the House is in session. Its removal to a lower pedestal means the House has resolved itself into a Committee of the Whole House on the State of the Union. Thus Members can see whether the House is in session or in committee. These signals are important because 218 Members constitute a quorum for action in the House and only 100 when the House is assembled in the Committee of the Whole. William Adams of New York reproduced this 46-inch Mace in 1841 from the design of its predecessor which the British destroyed by fire in 1814. It is a superb example of the silversmith's art, but cost the U.S. only $400. Today it is worth much more and historically and sentimentally it is beyond value. In the background on the marble wall is the fasces—rods and ax—symbolizing the authority of the ancient Roman magistrates, a graphic tradition that lives with us today.

Mace, symbol of authority in the House of Representatives.

The House

This is the Chamber in the House of Representatives where the President addresses a joint session of Congress. The Speaker of the House and the President of the Senate sit on the top dais in this set of three. The President, ministers, kings, diplomats, heads of state and public personalities of the first magnitude, in addressing a joint gathering of Members of the House and Senate in this Chamber, speak from the intermediary dais.*

In back is the flag of the United States. On the left of the Speaker's desk is the portrait of Washington, on the right the portrait of Lafayette, both full length. Above the clock is the gallery for the press. In the other galleries, the heavy television, newsreel and photographic equipment of the communications industry is located. This Chamber has three times the

floor area of the British House of Commons and is the largest national parliamentary room in the world. Here for the verdict of Congress were heard the Presidential messages that took the country into war, mobilizing 4,355,000 men in World War I and more than 16,000,000 in World War II.

The flag behind the Speaker, the brass fasces on either side of the flag, the American eagle surrounded by 50 stars in the center of the ceiling, and the colorful seals of each State forming the border decoration of the ceiling are symbols of our freedom in this historic Chamber that the House has occupied since 1857.

In 1973, an electronic voting system was installed to expedite the voting process. Components of this system are located on the walls behind and above the Speaker.

Electronic voting board located on the walls behind and above the Speaker.

*Only the President of the United States may address Congress in joint *session.* Any other occasion wherein notables address the Congress is referred to as a joint *meeting.*

The Speaker

*Foremost Man of His Party
in the House
The Speaker of the House
is Third in Line and
Second in Succession
to the Presidency*

It would do no violence to the truth to call the Speaker of the House the second most powerful office holder in the U.S. Government, surpassed only by the President. In fact, the Presidential Succession Act of 1947 places the Speaker second in line in succession to the Presidency, behind only the Vice-President, whose assumption to that office is required by the Constitution.

Visits with President
Jimmy Carter at the White
House are a routine item
on the Speaker's weekly
agenda.

Selecting a Speaker

In the early days the Speaker was elected by ballot, but since 1839 all have been chosen by roll call or voice vote. The election of the Speaker is traditionally the first order of business upon the convening of a new Congress.

The choosing of the Speaker has undergone a few significant changes over the past 190 years. Only relatively senior Members with 20-plus years of experience have been elected Speaker in this century. From 1789 to 1896, each new Speaker averaged only seven years of experience in Congress. Once elected, a Speaker is customarily re-elected as long as his party remains in the majority and he retains his Congressional seat.

Although the election officially occurs on the floor of the House, modern-day Speakers are actually decided upon when the majority party meets in caucus on the eve of a new Congress. Despite the forgone conclusion of the contest, the minority party also nominates its candidate who, upon losing, becomes minority leader. Since the 1930s, service in the lesser party leadership posts, such as majority and minority whip, majority and minority leader, have become stepping stones to the Speakership.

The stability of the two party system in the modern era has led to a period of unbroken lines of succession in the leadership tracks of both parties. This has not always been the case, however. In 1855, more than 130 separate votes were required over a period of two months before a Speaker was finally chosen. In 1859, only four years later, the House balloted 44 times before choosing a first-term New Jersey Congressman for the Speakership—and he was defeated for re-election *to the House* after that one term!

Powers and Duties

The Constitution makes but scant reference to the office, prescribing in Article I, Section 2 that "the House of Representatives shall chuse [sic] their speaker". While the powers and duties of the Speaker are spelled out to some degree in the *Rules of the House,* the effectiveness of any particular Speaker has depended upon a great many intangibles: the speaker's own personal dynamism, the size of his majority in the House, his relationship with the executive branch, his ability to "get things done". Men of greatly differing styles and temperaments have served as Speaker. Freshmen, septuagenarians, dictators, tyrants, moderates, Southerners, Northerners, former Presidents, Vice-Presidents (and would-be Presidents) have all, at one time or another, served in the Speaker's Chair.

In the modern era, the many duties of the Speaker include presiding at the sessions of the House, announcing the order of business, putting questions to a vote, reporting the vote and deciding points of order. He appoints the chairmen of the Committee of the Whole and members of select and conference committees. He chooses Speakers pro tem and refers bills and reports to the appropriate committees and calendars. Although he is not constitutionally required to be an elected Member of the House, this *de facto* requirement assures that the Speaker also enjoys the privileges of ordinary House Members. He may, therefore, after stepping down from the Chair, vote and participate in debate on the floor.

Perhaps the duties of the Speaker were put most idealistically by the first "great" Speaker, Henry Clay, back in 1823. It was up to the Speaker to be prompt and impartial in deciding questions of order, to display "patience, good temper and courtesy" to every Member, and to make "the best arrangement and distribution of the talent of the House", in carrying out the country's business. Finally, Clay noted, the Speaker must "remain cool and unshaken amidst all the storms of debate, carefully guarding the preservation of the permanent laws and rules of the House from being sacrificed to temporary passions, prejudices or interests". But in fact the Speakership today is a partisan office. As Floyd Riddick, Parliamentarian Emeritus of the U.S. Senate, has commented, "tradition and unwritten law require that the Speaker apply the rules of the House consistently, yet in the twilight zone a large area exists where he may exercise great discrimination and where he has many opportunities to apply the rules to his party's advantage".

Triple Personality

The Speaker of the House is a triple personality, being a Member of the House, its presiding officer and leader of the majority party in the Chamber. As a Member of the House he has the right to cast his vote on all questions, unlike the President of the Senate (the Vice President of the United States) who has no vote except in the case of a tie. Usually, however, the Speaker does not exercise his right to vote except to break a tie or when he desires to make his position known on a measure before the House. As a Member, he also has the right to leave the Chair and participate in debate on the House floor as the elected Representative of his district.

As presiding officer of the House, the Speaker interprets the rules that the House has adopted for guidance. In this matter he is customarily bound by precedents, created by prior decisions of the Chair. Appeals are usually in order from decisions of the Chair, but seldom occur. When they are taken, the Chair is usually sustained. The Speaker's power of recognition is partially limited by House rules and conventions that fix the time for considerations of various classes of bills.

He has discretion in choosing the Members he will recognize to make motions to suspend the rules on days when such motions are in order. The rules of the House may be suspended by two-thirds vote on the first and third Mondays of the month, the Tuesdays immediately following those days, and the last six days of the session.

As a party leader, the Speaker had certain additional powers prior to 1910: to appoint all standing committees and to name their chairmen; to select members of the Rules Committee; and from 1858 to serve as its chairman. His political power evolved gradually during the nineteenth century and peaked under the leadership of former Speaker Joseph Cannon.

In 1910, the House cut back some of the Speaker's power. They removed him from the Rules Committee, stripped him of his power to appoint the standing House committees and their chairmen and restricted his former right of recognition. These actions were not directed so much against the principle of leadership as against the concentration of power in the hands of a single individual.

Three Speakers gather at the Capitol—Carl Albert of Oklahoma, Thomas P. O'Neill, Jr. of Massachusetts and John W. McCormack of Massachusetts.

The Speaker (center) meets with Majority Leader, Jim Wright of Texas (left) and Minority Leader John J. Rhodes of Arizona (right) to discuss legislation.

Biography in Brief of Speaker Thomas P. O'Neill, Jr.

The Speaker is constantly speaking around the United States. Here he speaks for a colleague in Philadelphia.

Thomas Phillip "Tip" O'Neill, Jr., of Massachusetts' Eighth District was elected 47th Speaker of the U.S. House of Representatives January 4, 1977.

Speaker O'Neill was born in Cambridge, Massachusetts on December 9, 1912, son of Thomas P. O'Neill, who had been a bricklayer and later City Councilman, and the former Rose Ann Tolan. He was educated at St. John's Parochial School, and Boston College from which he was graduated in 1936. He worked in the insurance business but government and politics were his main occupation.

At 14 he was campaigning for Al Smith for President, and he ran for the Cambridge City Council while still a senior at Boston College. He lost, but a year later was elected to the Massachusetts House of Representatives. During his 16 years in the State House on Beacon Hill, he was chosen the first Democratic Speaker in the history of the Commonwealth of Massachusetts. After four years as State House Speaker, he was elected to Congress to succeed John F. Kennedy, who was moving to the U.S. Senate. In Washington, he quickly became a protégé of John W. McCormack and after a term on the Merchant Marine and Fisheries Committee, he became the second sophomore Congressman in history to be named to the powerful Rules Committee.

He was appointed Majority Whip in 1971 and was unanimously elected Majority Leader in 1973 and again in 1975. In 1977, he was elected without opposition as Speaker. He is the Eighth Speaker from Massachusetts, a record.

Speaker O'Neill is a determined golfer, card player and sports fan. He was nicknamed for James Edward O'Neill, of the old St. Louis Browns baseball team who compiled a .492 batting average in 1887 by tipping off foul balls until he won walks, which used to count as hits. When he is not in the Speaker's Chair presiding, he is usually found on the House floor talking with his colleagues about the problems of the day.

He is married to the former Mildred Anne Miller. They have five children.

Speaker O'Neill relaxes at his favorite recreation—golf. Weekends find him at the public and private links in Washington or Massachusetts.

Gavel in hand, the Speaker is the presiding officer in the House, the highest legislative position in the land.

Walking the beach at his home on Cape Cod, winter or summer, is a real pleasure for the Speaker.

IN GOD WE TRUST

Millie O'Neill has the Speaker's attention at the annual Democratic Dinner in Washington.

Vice President Walter F. Mondale of Minnesota (left) the presiding officer of the Senate and Speaker Thomas P. O'Neill, Jr., of Massachusetts exchange a few words prior to joint session of Congress.

Foreign dignitaries pay courtesy calls on the Speaker. Here, a visitor chats in the Speaker's office.

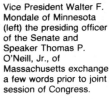

Three very good friends meet at the Capitol (left to right) Former Speaker John W. McCormack of Massachusetts, the late Vice President Hubert H. Humphrey of Minnesota and Speaker Thomas P. O'Neill, Jr. of Massachusetts.

Former Speakers

Frederick A. C. Muhlenberg, Pennsylvania: The first Speaker of the House of Representatives. He served during both the First and Third Congresses, April 1, 1789, to March 3, 1791, and December 2, 1793, to March 3, 1795.

Jonathan Trumbull, Connecticut: Second to occupy the Speakership of the House. He presided over Second Congress from October 24, 1791, to March 2, 1793.

Jonathan Dayton, New Jersey: Speaker, Fourth, and first session of Fifth Congresses, December 7, 1795, to March 3, 1797, and May 15, 1797, to July 10, 1797.

Theodore Sedgwick, Massachusetts: Speaker, Sixth Congress, December 2, 1799, to March 3, 1801.

82

Nathaniel Macon, North Carolina: Speaker, Seventh, Eighth, and Ninth Congresses, December 7, 1801, to March 3, 1807.

Joseph B. Varnum, Massachusetts: Speaker for Tenth and Eleventh Congresses, October 26, 1807, to March 3, 1811.

Henry Clay, Kentucky: Speaker, Twelfth and Thirteenth, second session Fourteenth, Fifteenth, first session of the Sixteenth, and Eighteenth Congresses, November 4, 1811, to January 19, 1814, December 4, 1815, to October 28, 1820, December 1, 1823, to March 3, 1825.

Langdon Cheves, South Carolina: Elected Speaker during second session of Thirteenth Congress, January 19, 1814, to March 3, 1815.

John W. Taylor, New York: Speaker, second session Sixteenth Congress, and Nineteenth Congress, November 15, 1820, to March 3, 1821, and December 5, 1825, to March 3, 1827.

Philip P. Barbour, Virginia: Speaker, Seventeenth Congress, December 4, 1821, to March 3, 1823.

Andrew Stevenson, Virginia: Speaker, Twentieth, Twenty-first, Twenty-second, and first session Twenty-third Congresses from December 3, 1827, to June 30, 1834.

John Bell, Tennessee: Speaker, second session Twenty-third Congress, from June 2, 1834, to March 3, 1835.

James K. Polk, Tennessee: Speaker, Twenty-fourth and Twenty-fifth Congresses from December 7, 1835, to March 3, 1839. Former Governor of Tennessee and eleventh President of the United States.

Robert M. T. Hunter, Virginia: Speaker, Twenty-sixth Congress, December 16, 1839, to March 3, 1841.

John White, Kentucky: Speaker of the Twenty-seventh Congress, May 31, 1841, to March 3, 1843.

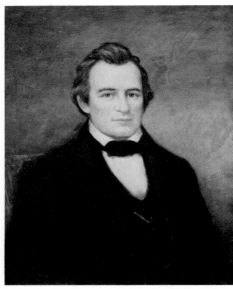

John W. Jones, Virginia: Speaker, Twenty-eighth Congress, December 4, 1843, to March 3, 1845.

John Wesley Davis, Indiana: Speaker of the Twenty-ninth Congress, December 1, 1845, to March 3, 1847.

Robert C. Winthrop, Massachusetts: Speaker, Thirtieth Congress, December 6, 1847, to March 3, 1849.

Howell G. Cobb, Georgia: Speaker, Thirty-first Congress, December 22, 1849, to March 3, 1851.

Linn Boyd, Kentucky: Speaker, Thirty-second, Thirty-third Congresses, December 1, 1851, to March 3, 1855.

Nathaniel P. Banks, Massachusetts: Speaker, Thirty-fourth Congress, February 2, 1856, to March 3, 1857.

James L. Orr, South Carolina: Speaker, Thirty-fifth Congress, December 7, 1857, to March 3, 1859.

William Pennington, New Jersey: Speaker, Thirty-sixth Congress, February 1, 1860, to March 3, 1861.

Galusha A. Grow, Pennsylvania: Speaker, Thirty-seventh Congress, July 4, 1861, to March 3, 1863.

Schuyler Colfax, Indiana: Speaker, Thirty-eighth, through the Fortieth Congresses, from December 7, 1863, to March 3, 1869.

Theodore M. Pomeroy, New York: Speaker last day of Fortieth Congress and served one day, March 3, 1869.

James G. Blaine, Maine: Speaker of the Forty-first through the Forty-third Congresses, from March 4, 1869, to March 3, 1875.

Michael C. Kerr, Indiana: Speaker, Forty-fourth Congress, first session, from December 6, 1875, to August 19, 1876.

Samuel J. Randall, Pennsylvania: Speaker, second session of Forty-fourth through the Forty-sixth Congresses, from December 4, 1876, to March 3, 1881.

J. Warren Keifer, Ohio: Speaker, Forty-seventh Congress, December 5, 1881, to March 3, 1883.

John G. Carlisle, Kentucky: Speaker, Forty-eighth through the Fiftieth Congresses, December 3, 1883, to March 3, 1889.

Thomas B. Reed, Maine: Speaker, Fifty-first, Fifty-fourth, Fifty-fifth Congresses, December 2, 1889, to March 2, 1891, and from December 2, 1895, to March 3, 1899.

Charles F. Crisp, Georgia: Speaker, Fifty-second and Fifty-third Congresses from December 8, 1891, to March 3, 1895.

David B. Henderson, Iowa: Speaker, Fifty-sixth and Fifty-seventh Congresses, from December 4, 1899, to March 3, 1903.

Joseph G. Cannon, Illinois: Speaker, Fifty-eighth through Sixty-first Congresses, from November 9, 1903, to March 3, 1911.

Champ Clark, Missouri: Speaker, Sixty-second through Sixty-fifth Congresses, from April 4, 1911, to March 3, 1919.

Frederick H. Gillett, Massachusetts: Speaker, Sixty-sixth through Sixty-eighth Congresses, from May 19, 1919, to March 3, 1925.

Nicholas Longworth, Ohio: Speaker, Sixty-ninth through Seventy-first Congresses, from December 7, 1925, to March 3, 1931.

John Nance Garner, Texas: Speaker, Seventy-second Congress, from December 7, 1931, to March 3, 1933. He later served as Vice President.

Henry T. Rainey, Illinois: Speaker, Seventy-third Congress, from March 9, 1933, to June 18, 1934.

Joseph W. Byrns, Tennessee: Speaker, Seventy-fourth Congress, from January 3, 1935, to June 4, 1936.

William B. Bankhead, Alabama: Elected Speaker during the Seventy-fourth Congress, served through the Seventy-sixth Congress, June 4, 1936, to September 15, 1940.

Sam Rayburn, Texas: Elected Speaker during the 76th Congress, served through the 79th Congress, then the 81st and 82d Congresses, and 84th through 87th Congresses (died after first session) from Sept. 16, 1940 to Jan. 3, 1947, Jan. 3, 1949 to July 7, 1952, and Jan. 5, 1955 to Nov. 16, 1961.

Joseph W. Martin, Jr., Massachusetts: Speaker, Eightieth Congress and Eighty-third Congress, from January 3, 1947, to December 31, 1948, and January 3, 1953, to December 2, 1954 or August 20, 1954.

John W. McCormack, Massachusetts: Speaker, second session, Eighty-seventh Congress through Ninety-first Congress, from January 10, 1962, to January 2, 1971.

Carl Albert, Oklahoma: Speaker, Ninety-second through Ninety-fourth Congresses, from January 21, 1971, to January 3, 1977.

House Leadership

In his formal office in the Capitol (H-204) Speaker Thomas P. O'Neill of Massachusetts goes over the day's schedule with his top staff assistants, Gary G. Hymel (left), Delores C. Snow and Leo E. Diehl.

The Democratic Leadership of the House of Representatives for the 96th Congress (left to right) Chief Deputy Majority Whip Dan Rostenkowski of Illinois; Majority Whip John Brademas of Indiana; Majority Leader James C. Wright of Texas; Speaker Thomas P. O'Neill, Jr. of Massachusetts; and Chairman, Democratic Caucus, Thomas I. Foley of Washington.

At the beginning of each Congress, the Leadership of the House of Representatives is elected. The Constitution authorizes the House to elect a Speaker. Each party caucus also elects its party leader. Under the tradition of the two party system in this country, the leader of the party with the largest number of Members becomes the Majority Leader. The Minority Leader is invariably the Member nominated by the minority party for the Speaker.

The Majority Leader works very closely with the Speaker in developing the party's position on major policy issues. He almost always has represented a different geographic area of the country from the Speaker. He consults with committee chairmen and urges them to move legislation which the party considers important.

Each party also appoints a whip and assistant whips to assist the floor leader in execution of the party's leg-

islative program. The main job of the whips is to canvas party members on a pending issue and give the floor leader an accurate estimate of the support or opposition expected on a bill. The term "whip" refers to the responsibility of these Members to pressure the other Members of their party to the floor for key votes.

In recent years the majority party has revitalized the Caucus of its Members and the Chairman of the Caucus, elected by his party colleagues, has become an important part of the leadership structure.

Usually considered as part of the "Leadership" are the chairmen of the twenty-two committees of the House. Until the Congressional reforms in 1975 the Chairmen achieved their status solely by virtue of their seniority. Currently, chairmen are elected by the majority party Caucus, by secret ballot. Committee Chairmen are nominated by the Steering and Policy Committee composed of House leaders, their nominees and Members elected by the Caucus on a regional basis.

House Minority Leader John J. Rhodes of Arizona confers in his Capitol Office H–232 with Clara Posey, Executive Secretary to the Minority Leader.

The Republican Leadership of the House of Representatives for the 96th Congress (front row, left to right) Minority Whip Robert H. Michel of Illinois; Minority Leader John J. Rhodes of Arizona; Conference Chairman Samuel L. Devine of Ohio; (back row, left to right) National Republican Congressional Committee Chairman Guy Vander Jagt of Michigan; Conference Secretary Clair Burgener of California; Policy Chairman E. G. (Bud) Shuster of Pennsylvania; Conference Vice Chairman Jack Edwards of Alabama; Ranking Minority Member, Rules Committee, James H. Quillen of Tennessee and Research Chairman Trent Lott of Mississippi.

House Minority Whip
Robert H. Michel of Illinois
confers with his personal
Secretary Carol Dearden.

Representative
Thomas S. Foley
of Washington,
Chairman,
House Democratic Caucus

Representative
Samuel L. Devine of Ohio,
Chairman of the Republican
Conference Committee.

House Majority Leader James C. Wright of Texas in his Capitol Office (H–148) with Executive Assistant Craig Raupe (left) and Executive Secretary Katherine Mitchell.

House Chief Deputy Whip Dan Rostenkowski in his Capitol office (H–115) with his Administrative Assistant James C. Haley, Jr.

House Majority Whip John Brademas of Indiana in his Capitol office (H–107) with Legislative Assistant Susan Osann.

93

Elected Officers of the House

At the beginning of each Session of Congress both bodies, by Majority vote, elect the officers whose responsibility it is to keep the House and Senate operating smoothly. These persons are not Members of the Congress. The House elects the Clerk of the House, the Sergeant at Arms, the Doorkeeper, and the Postmaster of the House.

Clerk of the House

This office has a broad range of legislative and administrative duties; these include presiding at the opening of each new Congress, pending the election of the Speaker; receiving the credentials of Members; compiling the Official Role of Representatives-elect; taking all votes and certifying passage of bills; processing all legislation; maintaining, printing and distributing documents relating to the legislative activity. The Clerk also receives all official communications during recess or adjournment periods.

A number of internal budgeting, disbursing, accounting and housekeeping responsibilities are also assigned to the Clerk. This officer is assisted by the Offices of Finance, Supply Service, Equipment Service, and Records and Registration.

Sergeant at Arms of the House

This office enforces the rules of the House and maintains decorum during sessions of the House. The Sergeant at Arms also is in charge of the Mace, the symbol of legislative power and authority.

Maintaining the general security of the House buildings and the Capitol is his major responsibility.

This officer alternates with the Senate Sergeant at Arms as Chairman of the Capitol Police Board and the Capitol Guide Board. Another major responsibility is management of the House bank which disburses Members' salaries and travel expenses.

Edmund L. Henshaw, Jr.,
Clerk of the House,
presiding at the opening of
the 96th Congress pending
the election of the Speaker
of the House.

Edmund Henshaw, Jr.
Clerk of the House

Kenneth R. Harding
Sergeant at Arms

Doorkeeper of the House

Physical arrangements for joint sessions and joint meetings of the Congress, announcements of messages from the President and the Senate, announcement of the arrival of the President when he addresses Congress in person, escorting dignitaries visiting the Capitol—those are the tasks the public sees the Doorkeeper performing. In addition, he supervises the doormen stationed at each entrance to the House floor and House gallery; supervises the pages; operates the Document Room which provides copies of House bills, laws, committee reports, and other documents to the Members, the media and the public on request. Under his jurisdiction are the staff members serving the media galleries and the Members' cloakrooms. He also distributes authorized publications such as the Congressional Directory and copies of the U.S. Codes to the Members and their staffs.

Postmaster of the House

The primary duty of the Postmaster is to provide mail pickup and delivery service to the House wing of the Capitol, the House office buildings and the House annexes. Four post offices are under his jurisdiction and provide the usual counter service.

The Postmaster also provides a mail security system which scans every piece of incoming mail. Over 50 million incoming letters and publications are processed annually. Another 50 million or more communications such as the *Congressional Record*, news releases, agency publications also are handled annually.

Robert V. Rota, Postmaster of the House, goes over the day's schedule with one of his assistants.

Robert V. Rota
Postmaster

James T. Molloy
Doorkeeper

One of the numerous duties of James T. Molloy, Doorkeeper of the House, is to supervise the pages.

Kenneth R. Harding (right), Sergeant at Arms of the House with Inspector Herbert Price of the Capitol Police. Behind them is the Mace of the House of Representatives which the House Sergeant of Arms is responsible for among his many duties.

Pages of the United States Congress

Pages checking legislative calendar.

The practice of employing pages to serve the Members of both the House and Senate, primarily as messengers, has evolved since the origin of the Federal government in 1789.

House pages are under the supervision of the Doorkeeper; Senate pages of the Sergeant at Arms. They deliver documents and messages and run errands for the Members. Visitors are intrigued by the bench pages who sit on the rostrum steps and assist the Members during the session. Others are assigned to the Cloakroom, the Speaker's office, and the Senate Majority and Minority Leaders.

Until 1971, only males were employed as pages. The first Senate female pages were appointed in May, 1971 by Senators Jacob Javits of New York and Charles Percy of Illinois. Former Speaker Carl Albert of Oklahoma appointed the first official female House page in 1973.

Pages are selected by the Senators or Representatives whose seniority permits this privilege. The "patron" agrees to be responsible for the safety and conduct of pages he or she appoints. Senate pages may be between the ages of 14 and 17; House pages are limited to those who are 16 to 18, or who are juniors or seniors in high school. They must maintain at least a C average and be of good character. Pages live in rooming houses or with relatives in the area, since repeated efforts over the years have failed to provide a dormitory-education facility.

The pages attend the Capitol Page school currently located in the Library of Congress. They attend four or five 45-minute classes, five days a week, beginning at 6:45 a.m. and continuing until 9:45 a.m. The four year high school is accredited by the Middle States Association of Colleges and Secondary Schools. The curriculum is college preparatory, since 78 percent of the pages go on to college. There are six teachers and a principal-counseler, a basketball team, yearbook, school paper, student counsel and social and extra-curricular activities.

Numerous government officials, Members of the House of Representatives and Senate, officials of the House and Senate began their careers as Congressional pages. Three incumbent Representatives and one incumbent Senator are former pages: Representative Robert Bauman of Maryland; Representative John Dingell, Jr., of Michigan; Representative Jon Hinson of Mississippi; and Senator David H. Pryor of Arkansas.

Representative
Robert E. Bauman of
Maryland

Representative
John D. Dingell of
Michigan

Representative
Jon Hinson of
Mississippi

Senator
David H. Pryor of
Arkansas

Pages receiving their assignments.

Pages on the steps of the Capitol.

Pages with the Speaker Thomas P. O'Neill, Jr., of Massachusetts.

Graduation day for Pages of the United States Congress.

Pages with Representative Carl D. Perkins of Kentucky, Chairman, Committee on Education and Labor.

Pages sorting United States flags which flew over the Capitol.

Senate Majority Leader Robert C. Byrd of West Virginia (right), with Joseph Stewart, Secretary to the Majority and pages in Senate cloakroom.

The United States Senate

*Official Portrait of the
United States Senate,
September 13, 1979.*

The Senate of the United States is the champion of the States and the co-equal partner of the House of Representatives. On the pediment of the Dirksen Senate Office Building are engraved in marble the words: "THE SENATE IS THE LIVING SYMBOL OF OUR UNION OF STATES."

There are 100 Senators, 2 from each of the States. They are elected for a term of 6 years by a rotating system of elections every 2 years so that "one-third may be chosen every second year". Sixteen times in its history, the Senate has proved to be a training ground for future Presidents of the United States.

The election of Senators by State legislatures, as originally provided in Article I of the Constitution, was abandoned in 1913 with the adoption of the Seventeenth Amendment, providing for direct vote by the people. The election of Senators by direct vote of the people associated the Senate more directly with the people and intensified the truly representative nature of the whole Congress. The Vice President of the United States, says the Constitution, "shall be President of the Senate, but shall have no vote, unless they be equally divided". Whether he wishes to vote or not in the event of such a tie, is a matter of choice with the Vice President himself.

The powers of the Senate overlap into the Judicial and Executive Branches. Thus, the Senate is required to confirm most of the President's appointments. The Senate also ratifies or rejects treaties negotiated by the President with foreign powers. While the House has the power of impeachment, it is the Senate that tries officials who are impeached, and has the aura and authority of a high court.

The Senate and the House enjoy the constitutional power to make their own rules of procedure. In fulfilling its legislative and informing functions, Senate debate is regulated by rules that are more fluid than the rules of the House. Any Senator may speak for as long as he pleases except when debate is limited by the adoption of a cloture motion or by the terms of a unanimous consent agreement.

Bills in the process of becoming law may come to the Senate from the House or go to the House from the Senate. They are thus subject to the advantage of a second look. This doublecheck affords each legislative body a certain appellate function over the other.

A conference of committees of the two Houses generally works out a mutually acceptable compromise on a bill in controversy. Then, passed by both Houses in this final form, it is ready for submission to the President for his signature. Thereupon it becomes law.

This liaison between the two Houses produces deeply considered decisions. It brings to common ground the thinking of the House and the Senate. It develops cooperation.

The end result of this two-way scrutiny of prospective legislation is that it helps to cut to a minimum the margins for error and misjudgment.

Inherent in the bicameral system is the fundamental principle that no State, without its consent, shall be deprived of its equal suffrage in the Senate. Texas or Alaska, New York or California whether dominant in geography, in population, in natural resources or in financial power, cannot in the Senate overwhelm such States, for instance, as Rhode Island or Delaware, Mississippi or Montana, or each other. The gallery section over the Vice President's rostrum is occupied by the members of the news media. The other 611 seats in the gallery are available for visitors and members of Senators' families who wish to observe the Senate in action.

Senate Majority Leader Robert Byrd of West Virginia accepts the latest edition of *Senate Procedure* by the author Senate Parliamentarian Emeritus Floyd Riddick.

Senate Chamber Desks

When British troops set the Capitol ablaze in 1814, they heavily damaged the Senate Chamber and destroyed its furnishings. As part of the renovation to reopen the Chamber in 1819, the Senate ordered 48 desks at a cost of $34 each from Thomas Constantine, a New York cabinetmaker, who also built the desks for the House of Representatives. Many of these desks remain in the Senate Chamber today, and desks of a similar design have been added as each new State entered the Union.

Over the years several modifications have been made to the desks, primarily to provide more room for the Senators. During much of the 19th century, a Senator's office was his desk on the Senate floor. Beginning in the 1830's three-inch high mahogany writing boxes were added to the desks. Hinged on the top, these writing boxes opened to provide additional space.

Not all Senators preferred the modification, and today one desk still does not have a writing box. This is the Webster desk, which supposedly Daniel Webster refused to have altered on the grounds that if his predecessor could have done without the additional space, so could he. None of Webster's successors have seen fit to abandon that stance. To match its height to the level of others in the Chamber, the desk is raised at its base. Webster had represented Massachusetts in the Senate but had been born in New Hampshire. For many years his desk was occupied by New Hampshire Senators Styles Bridges and Norris Cotton. In 1974, just before Cotton retired from the Senate, he secured adoption of a resolution (S. Res. 467, 93d Cong., 2d sess.) which required that the Webster desk always be assigned to the senior Senator from New Hampshire.

In the mid-nineteenth century mahogany shelves were added at the base of the desks. Later at the turn of the century the legs of the desks were enclosed with a metal grille connected to a plenum chamber below the floor which provided better ventilation. The sanders and inkwells on top of the desks have also undergone change. The original inkwells were made from clear cut glass, covered with square, flat tops that moved horizontally. In 1933, what remained of the original inkwells were replaced by containers with hinged covers because duplicates of the earlier design were no longer being manufactured.

Over the years the desks have been rearranged periodically, as new States sent Senators and as party representation increased and diminished. When additional desks were needed, they were generally contracted out, although the last four desks, for Alaska in 1959 and Hawaii in 1960, were built in the Senate carpentry shop.

The easiest method for tracing the heritage of each desk is to read the names written and carved inside the desk drawers. This appears to be a 20th century tradition, since, for the most part, the earliest recorded names date back only to the first decade of the century. It is possible that 19th century Senators also inscribed their names in the desks, but that these names may have been lost during the refinishing of the drawers.

One difficulty in tracing back the names into the 19th century is that the early Senate Doorkeepers kept such information a closely guarded secret. Isaac Bassett, page and Doorkeeper from 1831 through 1895, feared that relic hunters might destroy the furniture if they knew which pieces were Clay's, Calhoun's and Webster's. Bassett had reasonable cause for alarm, for in 1861 he had stopped the mutilation of one of the Chamber's most famous desks. In April 1861, when the Sixth Massachusetts Regiment was temporarily bivouacked in the Senate Chamber during a recess, Bassett entered the Chamber in time to hear the sound of splitting wood on the Democratic side. Rushing over he found a Union soldier bayonetting the desk vacated by Jefferson Davis, President of the Confederacy. "Stop that; stop that; what are you doing?" Bassett shouted. "That is not Jeff. Davis' desk, it belongs to the Government of the United States. You were sent here to protect Government property, and not to destroy it." Today, a small block of wood inlaid on the left side of the desk (currently occupied by Senator John C. Stennis (D.-Miss.)) covers the spot where the bayonet once struck.

The custom of dividing Senate desks by party is as old as the parties themselves, with Democrats traditionally sitting to the Presiding Officer's right and Republicans to his left. This division, however, has not always been so clear cut.

In the Old Senate Chamber, an equal number of desks were placed on either side of the aisle, without regard to party size. There was no hard rule as to placement, and during the 1840's and 1850's, some Democrats could be found sitting at random on the Whig side. When the Senate moved to its current Chamber in 1859, the practice of dividing the desks equally continued for several years.

The new Chamber was large enough to permit a more flexible seating arrangement, and, in 1877, the practice developed of moving desks back and forth across the center aisle to permit all Members of the majority party to sit together on the appropriate side. From time to time since then, however, one party has elected such an overwhelming majority that it has again become necessary to have majority Members sitting on the minority side. For instance, during the 60th Congress (1907–1909) ten Republicans sat on the Democratic side, while during the 75th Congress (1937–1939) 13 Democrats sat on the Republican side.

Such seating became known as the "Cherokee Strip," meaning that the overflow of majority party Senators were off their reservation. (The Cherokee Strip in Oklahoma referred to land belonging to neither the Indian Territory nor the States.)

The seating of the Majority and Minority leaders at the front row desks on either side of the center aisle is a relatively recent Senate tradition, dating back to 1927 for the Democrats and 1937 for the Republicans.

Daniel Webster's Desk.

101

The Majority Leader

The Majority Leader of the Senate is the closest counterpart of the Speaker of the House, although the Framers of the Constitution apparently did not foresee such a development.

The Constitution's only references to leadership posts in the Senate are contained in two passages of Article I, Section 3. One passage provides that the Vice President "shall be President of the Senate, but shall have no vote, unless they be equally divided" (Clause 4). The other passage provides that the "Senate shall choose . . . a President Pro Tempore, in the absence of the Vice President, or when he shall exercise the office of the President of the United States" (Clause 5). With few exceptions, the Senate has been reluctant to place substantial political power in these offices. It has instead entrusted power to the majority and minority leaders.

Historical studies attempting to explain the Senate's attitude toward these top offices have stressed the unwillingness of Senators to delegate power either to a non-member (the Vice President), or to a Member (the President Pro Tempore) who may preside only at times of the Vice President's absence. If the Vice President and President Pro Tempore are of different political parties, which has often been the case, the Vice President is able to neutralize the authority of the President Pro Tempore by merely assuming the chair. Consequently the Senate has vested the real leadership in its party floor leaders.

Selection

Emergence of readily recognizable floor leaders in the Senate did not occur until 1911–13. Designation of these positions was the culmination of an increasing party influence in the chamber which began around 1890. Before that time, leadership in the Senate was usually vested in powerful individuals or small factions of Senators.

In the early years of the twentieth century each party elected its own chairman for the party caucus, but no Senator was elected to be the Majority or Minority Leader as we know these offices today. The "caucus" was in charge of putting through the legislative program.

The Majority and Minority Leaders today are elected by a majority vote of all the Senators in their respective parties. The practice has been to choose the leaders for a two-year term at the beginning of each Congress. After the parties have held their elections, the selection is made known through the press or by announcement to the Senate.

Powers and Duties

The Majority Leader is the elected spokesman on the Senate floor for the majority party. The office is a political one, and was not created by the rules of the Senate even though the rules do confer certain powers on the Majority Leader.

The Legislative Reorganization Acts of 1946 and 1970, and more recent amendments to the Senate rules, have given certain unique authorities to the Majority Leader.

The Majority Leader is responsible for the enactment of his party's legislative program. His role is an integral

President Carter and Senate Majority Leader Rober C. Byrd of West Virginia discuss legislation at the White House.

part of the effective functioning of the machinery of the Senate. The Majority Leader must keep himself informed on national and international problems in addition to pending legislative matters. On the floor of the Senate he is charged by his party members to deal with all procedural questions in consultation with them and his party's policy-making bodies. In turn, he must keep his party colleagues informed as to proposed action on pending measures. In more recent years, the Majority Leader also has been responsible for the scheduling of legislation.

The Majority Leader acts as a clearinghouse for his party as to the status of pending legislation. He works with party members to secure cooperation and unity in carrying out the party's program. The leader or his designee remains on the floor at all times while the Senate is in session to see that the program is carried out to the party's satisfaction.

The Majority Leader (currently Democratic) is ex-officio chairman of all of the Party's policy making and organizational bodies—that is, the Democratic Conference, the Demo-

cratic Policy Committee, and the Democratic Steering Committee.

The Majority Leader almost invariably: (a) offers motions to recess or adjourn from day to day; (b) calls up the *sine die* adjournment resolution and other resolutions relating to adjournment, including resolutions and motions to adjourn for periods of several days; (c) makes motions to proceed to the consideration of all proposed legislation (bills and resolutions); and (d) proffers routine requests to accommodate the Senate, including orders to permit standing committees to meet while the Senate is in session, notwithstanding the provisions of the rule. These are the parliamentary means which enable the Senate to conduct its day-to-day business.

Through the years, the Majority Leader has made the motions to recess or adjourn from day to day, until it is now assumed to be virtually his prerogative.

The Majority Leader keeps in close touch with the Minority Leader as to proposed legislation to be brought up, the procedure to be followed, and the legislative contests to be staged.

In earlier years, even in the 20th

century, chairmen of committees usually submitted motions to proceed to the consideration of bills reported by their own committees. At the present time, however, nearly all such motions are made by the Majority Leader himself.

In summary, the Senate floor leader performs six basic functions of leadership. He is, or has the potential for being, the principal force in organizing the party, scheduling business for the Senate, promoting attendance on the floor, collecting and distributing information, persuading other Senators to unite on policy questions, and providing liaison with the White House.

President Room, located in (S–216) of the Capitol is the place many bills were signed by Presidents. Pictured behind the table used by President Lincoln and other chief executives of the United States stands Senate Minority Leader and Mrs. Howard Baker, Jr. of Tennessee (left) and Senate Majority Leader and Mrs. Robert C. Byrd of West Virginia talking with two of Washington's most distinguished reporters Joseph McCaffrey and Betty Beale.

Biography in Brief of the Majority Leader Robert C. Byrd

A pensive Majority Leader ponders the problems of the Nation—and the world.

Senator Robert Carlyle Byrd of West Virginia was elected United States Senate Majority Leader by his Democratic colleagues on January 4, 1977 and reelected unanimously in 1979.

The Senate's most powerful position was achieved by a man of remarkable initiative who has held more legislative elective offices than any other individual in the history of West Virginia.

Born Cornelius Calvin Sale, Jr., on November 20, 1917, in North Wilkesboro, North Carolina, he was sent to live with his aunt and uncle, Vlurma and Titus Byrd, of Stotesbury, West Virginia, after his mother died in the influenza epidemic of 1918. He thus acquired the name Robert Byrd from his adoptive parents.

Educated in West Virginia public schools, he graduated valedictorian of the 1934 class of Stotesbury's Mark Twain High School. Because of the depression, he could not afford to go to college. Later, however, he earned his law degree, graduating *cum laude* from American University in Washington, D.C., an accomplishment achieved by attending night school for 10 years while serving in the United States House of Representatives and Senate.

Senator Byrd, who was employed in a grocery store in southern West Virginia when he initially became interested in politics, was first elected to the West Virginia House of Delegates and later to the West Virginia Senate. He was elected to the United States House of Representatives in 1952, serving three terms before being elected to the United States Senate in 1958.

In the Senate, Senator Byrd sought and obtained a seat on the influential Appropriations Committee, and today also serves on the Judiciary and Rules and Administration Committees. In January 1967, Senator Byrd was elected Secretary of the Senate Democratic Conference and in 1971 was chosen Senate Majority Whip, a position he held until being elected Majority Leader.

In his present office, Senator Byrd is credited in a poll conducted by *U.S. News and World Report* with providing the leadership that enabled the United States Senate to attain its highest ranking in influence in the history of the annual survey.

The Majority Leader is an accomplished musician who is dedicated to preserving the Bluegrass and Appalachian mountain music that is so much a part of West Virginia's heritage. He plays the violin as a hobby, and has performed his music on various national television programs.

Senator Byrd is married to the former Erma Ora James. They have two daughters and six grandchildren.

The Majority Leader meets the Press.

A young Robert C. Byrd, (right), helps carry lunch pailes to the local boarding house in West Virginia.

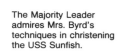

The Majority Leader admires Mrs. Byrd's techniques in christening the USS Sunfish.

The Majority Leader "does his homework".

Vice Premier Deng Xiao Ping of the People's Republic of China and the Majority Leader.

President Carter and the Majority Leader enjoy a relaxing moment at the White House.

Senator and Mrs. Byrd keep close contact with West Virginia voters, rain or shine.

Finance Committee Chairman, Senator Russell Long of Louisiana, confers with the Majority Leader on tax legislation.

Graduate of American University law school.

The Majority Leader plays the fiddle at a Democratic Dinner.

Former Majority Leaders

SHELBY M. CULLOM of Illinois: Majority Leader, 62nd Congress, April 4, 1911, to March 3, 1913.

JOHN W. KERN of Indiana: Majority Leader, 63rd and 64th Congresses, March 5, 1913, to March 3, 1917.

THOMAS S. MARTIN of Virginia: Majority Leader, 65th Congress, March 6, 1917, to March 3, 1919.

HENRY CABOT LODGE of Massachusetts: Majority Leader, 66th Congress through first session of 68th Congress, from March 4, 1919, to November 9, 1924.

CHARLES CURTIS of Kansas: the first to actually be called a "floor leader." He served as Majority Leader from the first session of the 68th Congress through the 70th Congress, from November 28, 1924, to March 3, 1929.

JAMES E. WATSON of Indiana: Majority Leader, 71st and 72nd Congresses from March 5, 1929, to March 3, 1933.

JOSEPH T. ROBINSON of Arkansas: Majority Leader, 73rd Congress through the first session of the 75th Congress, from March 4, 1933, to July 14, 1937.

ALBEN W. BARKLEY of Kentucky: Majority Leader, 75th Congress, first session, through 79th Congress, July 22, 1937, to January 3, 1947. He is a former Vice President of the U. S.

WALLACE H. WHITE, JR. of Maine: Majority Leader, 80th Congress, January 3, 1947, to January 3, 1949.

SCOTT W. LUCAS of Illinois: Majority Leader in the 81st Congress, January 20, 1949, to January 3, 1951.

ERNEST W. McFARLAND of Arizona: Majority Leader, 82nd Congress, February 22, 1951, to January 3, 1953.

ROBERT A. TAFT of Ohio: Majority Leader in the 83rd Congress, first session, from January 3, 1953, to July 31, 1953.

WILLIAM F. KNOWLAND of California, Majority Leader in the 83rd Congress, from August 4, 1953, to January 3, 1955.

LYNDON B. JOHNSON of Texas. This former U.S. President and Vice President served as Majority Leader from the 84th through the 86th Congresses, from January 3, 1955, to January 3, 1961.

MIKE MANSFIELD of Montana: Majority Leader from the 87th through the 94th Congresses, January 3, 1961, to January 3, 1977.

Senate Leadership

Senate Majority Leader, Robert C. Byrd of West Virginia discusses the legislative schedule with his Executive Secretary, Barbara Videnieks, (left), and Mary Jane Checchi, (center), Chief Counsel and Staff Director of the Democratic Policy Committee. The Majority Leader's office is located in Room S–208 of the Capitol.

The Democratic Leadership of the Senate (left to right), Majority Whip Alan Cranston of California; Secretary of Democratic Conference Daniel K. Inouye of Hawaii; President Pro Tempore Warren G. Magnuson of Washington; and Majority Leader Robert C. Byrd of West Virginia.

The Constitution requires that the Vice President is the President of the Senate. Since the Vice President is frequently not present in the Senate, except in the case of a close vote which may end in a tie, the Senate elects a President pro tempore, by custom, in recent decades, the most senior majority Member of the Senate. The President pro tempore is a key member of his party's policy-making body. He usually designates a more junior Senator to preside over daily sessions in his place. The President pro tempore also has the responsibility for the Legislative Counsel, a group of legal specialists who assist Senators in drafting bills.

Since the early days of the twentieth century, the Senate has, by custom developed the position of Majority Leader as a parallel in power to the Speaker of the House.

The real leader of the Senate is the Majority Leader. He is the legislative strategist and exercises considerable influence on committee assignments.

The Majority Leader is elected by the Senators who are members of the political party to which more than 50 percent of the Senators belong. The Senators of the party with the lesser number elect a Minority Leader.

In cooperation with their party organization, each Leader is responsible for the achievement of the legislative program. They manage the order in which legislation moves to passage and expedite noncontroversial legislation. They keep members of their

party informed regarding pending business. Each Leader is an ex-officio Member of his party's policymaking and organizing body. Each is aided by an assistant Leader, called the Whip, as in the House, and by the Majority or Minority Secretary, who are professional staff administrators, but not Members of the Senate.

Each of the two major parties in the Senate is organized differently. The Democrats have a caucus which nominates the Leaders, elects the Steering Committee and approves Steering Committee nominations for Committee Chairmen. The Steering Committee nominates Committee Chairmen and assigns party members to Committees. The Democratic Policy Committee develops legislative policy and positions.

The Republican Senators comprise the Republican Conference which elects the Minority Leader and deals with procedural matters. The Conference Committees assign party members to Committees. They also elect the Republican Policy Committee which handles the research and policy determination function of the party.

Senate Minority Leader Howard H. Baker of Tennessee, far right, in his Capitol office (S–230) with chief assistants, Laura Nell Triplett, Executive Secretary; William Hildenbrand, Secretary for the Minority; and James Cannon, Administrative Assistant.

Republican Leadership for the 96th Congress (left to right); Senators Ted Stevens of Alaska, Minority Whip; Howard H. Baker, Jr. of Tennessee, Minority Leader; Milton R. Young of North Dakota, Republican Dean; Bob Packwood of Oregon, Chairman, Republican Conference; John Tower of Texas, Chairman, Republican Policy Committee; Edwin (Jake) Garn of Utah, Secretary, Republican Conference; and H. John Heinz of Pennsylvania, Chairman, Republican Senatorial Campaign Committee.

Senate Majority Whip Alan
D. Cranston of California,
left, in his Capitol office
(S-148) with
Administrative Assistant
Roy F. Greenway.

Senator Daniel K. Inouye
of Hawaii
Secretary
Senate Democratic
Conference.

Senator Edwin (Jake) Garn
of Utah
Secretary
Senate Republican
Conference.

Senator Warren G.
Magnuson of Washington,
President Pro Tempore of
the Senate.

Senator John G. Tower of Texas, Chairman, Republican Policy Committee.

Senator H. John Heinz of Pennsylvania Chairman Republican Senatorial Campaign Committee.

Senate Republican Conference Chairman, Bob Packwood of Oregon reviews floor statement with his Administrative Assistant Mimi Weyforth.

Senator Ted Stevens of Alaska, Minority Whip of the Senate.

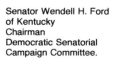

Senator Wendell H. Ford of Kentucky Chairman Democratic Senatorial Campaign Committee.

Elected Officers of the Senate

At the beginning of each session the Senate elects its officers for a two year term. These officers are the Secretary of the Senate, the Sergeant at Arms and the Majority and Minority Secretaries. The Chaplain is also elected.

Secretary of the Senate

The primary duty of this officer is for the legislative administration of the Senate. He is custodian of the Senate Seal; administers oaths of office; certifies passage of legislation, ratification of treaties and confirmation or rejection of Presidential nominations. He is assisted in his legislative administration by a wide variety of experts, including the Parliamentarian, Legislative Clerk, Office of Classified National Security Information, Journal Clerk, Disbursing Officer, Senate Librarian, Senate Historian and official reporters, among others. He also is a member of the Federal Election Commission, the Federal Council on the Arts and Humanities and serves as Executive Secretary to the Commission on Arts and Antiquities of the Senate.

Sergeant at Arms of the Senate

The responsibility of the Sergeant at Arms of the Senate is primarily to enforce the rules of the Senate and maintain decorum. In addition, he supervises the computer and micrographic centers, Senate post offices, press galleries, service department, recording studio, telephone services and janitorial services. He rotates with the House Sergeant at Arms as chairman of the Capitol Police Board and the Capitol Guide Board. He also is the protocol officer of the Senate including the announcement of the arrival of the President and other dignitaries.

F. Nordy Hoffman,
Sergeant at Arms

Senate Majority Leader,
Robert C. Byrd of West
Virginia is briefed by
J. Walter Stewart,
Secretary to the Majority.

J. Stanley Kimmitt,
Secretary of the Senate

Secretary to the Majority and the Minority

The Secretary to the Majority and the Secretary to the Minority are also elected officers of the Senate. Their duties are similar—primarily to supervise the majority and minority cloakroom, obtain pair votes for Senators as requested, brief Senators on votes and issues under consideration, poll the Senators at the request of the Leadership and in general serving the Senators who comprise the majority and minority.

J. Walter Stewart,
Secretary to the Majority

Secretary to the Minority,
William F. Hildenbrand
reviews the legislative
schedule with Howard
Green, Assistant Secretary
to the Minority.

William F. Hildenbrand,
Secretary to the Minority

Senate Sergeant at Arms,
F. Nordy Hoffman informs
Pages on the Senates
legislative schedule.

Secretary of the Senate,
J. Stanley Kimmitt discusses
matters of the Senate with
his administrative assistant
Gail Martin.

Five Outstanding Senators

Adjacent to the Senate Chamber on the second floor of the Senate wing of the Capitol is the Senate Reception Room.

Aside from "real live Senators" who leave the Senate floor to confer with constituents, government officials, lobbyists and visitors during sessions of the Senate, the most impressive feature of the Senate Reception Room is the series of portraits of five former U.S. Senators selected as outstanding among all the persons who served in the U.S. Senate before 1959, the year the portraits were placed in the five hitherto empty spaces.

A Special Senate Committee on the Senate Reception Room was established by a resolution of the 84th Congress. Senator John F. Kennedy (D-Massachusetts) was named Chairman. The other members of the Committee were: Senators Richard B. Russell (D-Georgia), Mike Mansfield (D-Montona), John W. Bricker (R-Ohio), and Styles Bridges (R-New Hamp-

Senate Minority Leader Ted Stevens (Alaska); Majority Whip Alan Cranston (Calif.); Majority Leader Robert C. Byrd (W. Va.) and Minority Leader Howard H. Baker, Jr. (Tenn.) meet prior to Senate going into session in the Senate Reception Room (S–213) just off the Senate floor.

shire). The committee was charged with the duty of selecting "five outstanding persons from among all persons, but not a living person, who have served as Members of the Senate since the formation of the Government of the United States whose painting shall be placed in the five unfilled spaces in the Senate reception room".

The Chairman of the Special Committee, Senator John F. Kennedy, was the chief organizer and proponent of the project to select the outstanding senators. During long months of convalescence from back surgery to correct damage from injuries received in WWII, Senator Kennedy studied extensively the lives and contributions of great Americans who in times of decision placed the national good above popular opinion. His book, *Profiles in Courage* was the forerunner of his work on the Special Committee. The Senate resolution also authorized the Committee to consult with "historians and other sources, including the general public as it deems advisable".

The criteria recommended by the advisory committee provided that the five Senators should be chosen without regard for their services in other offices, that they should be distinguished for acts of statesmanship transcending party and State lines, and that their leadership in national thought and constitutional interpretation be considered as well as in legislation.

The Committee reported in May 1, 1957. The report stressed that those selected were "not necessarily the five greatest Senators; nor the most blameless or irreproachable ones, nor models of contemporary behavior. Allowances must be made, moreover, of the times, the morals, and the practices of the period in which each served; and political and policy differences should not diminish their claim to the label outstanding."

The artists commissioned by the Senate were Arthur Conrad for Calhoun, Allyn Cox for Clay, Chester La Follette for LaFollette, Dean C. Keller for Taft and Adrian Lamb for Webster.

The five outstanding senators of the past were chosen by a Special Committee, and approved by the entire Senate

Clay

Senator
Henry Clay,
of Kentucky, who
served in the Senate
1806–7, 1810–11, 1831–42, 1849–52

Webster

Senator
Daniel Webster,
of Massachusetts,
who served in the Senate
1827–41, 1845–50

Calhoun

Senator
John C. Calhoun,
of South Carolina, who
served in the Senate
1832–43, 1845–50

La Follette

Senator
Robert M.
La Follette, Sr., of Wisconsin,
who served in the Senate 1906–25.

Taft

Senator
Robert A. Taft, of
Ohio, who served in the
Senate 1939–53

Vice President and President of the Senate

The Vice President, who is the constitutionally designated presiding officer of the Senate, is a unique figure in our government. He is the only official with duties both in the executive and legislative branches. For many years the Vice President was not much more than "the man in the wings" waiting to fill the void should a vacancy occur in the presidency.

Since Harry Truman's presidency, however, the role of the Vice President has been steadily expanded and now even more than ever, the Vice President does indeed play a key role in our system of Government.

The Constitution states the key role of the President of the Senate as follows: "The Vice President of the United States shall be President of the

The Vice President meets at the White House with the President, Congressional Leaders and key staff members (left to right) Speaker of the House, Thomas P. O'Neill, Jr., of Massachusetts; President Jimmy Carter; Senate Majority Leader, Robert C. Byrd of West Virginia; House Democratic Caucus Chairman, Thomas S. Foley of Washington; Assistant to the President for Domestic Affairs and Policy, Stuart E. Eizenstat; Assistant to the Vice President for Congressional Relations, William Smith; House Majority Leader James C. Wright of Texas; Vice President Walter F. Mondale; Senate Majority Whip, Alan D. Cranston of California, and House Chief Deputy Whip, Dan Rostenkowski of Illinois.

Vice President Walter F. Mondale and Mrs. Mondale in the Ceremonial Office of the Vice President, just off the Senate floor in room S–212 of the Capitol. The desk, mirror, and fireplace date from the room's first occupancy in 1859.

The Vice President with friend and former Senator Muriel Humphrey, wife of the late Vice President Hubert H. Humphrey of Minnesota.

Senate, but shall have no vote, unless they be equally divided." And again the Constitution stipulates: "The Senate shall chuse [sic] their other Officers, and also a President pro tempore, in the Absence of the Vice President, or when he shall exercise the Office of President of the United States."

Many well-known figures in American history—John Adams, Thomas Jefferson, Martin Van Buren, Theodore Roosevelt, Harry S. Truman, Lyndon B. Johnson, Richard Nixon, and others—have risen from the Presidency of the Senate, to top leadership as President of the United States. Twelve former Vice Presidents have later served in the White House.

Vice President Walter F. Mondale of Minnesota is no stranger to the Capitol having served in the U.S. Senate from late 1964 to just a few days prior to becoming the 42nd Vice President of the United States in January 1977. Prior to his service in the Senate he was Attorney General of the State of Minnesota.

Speaker of the House of Representatives, Thomas P. O'Neill, Jr., of Massachusetts administers the oath of office to the 42d Vice President of the United States, Walter F. Mondale of Minnesota as Mrs. Mondale holds Bible.

Former Vice Presidents

John Adams, Massachusetts, a Federalist, first President of the Senate and Vice President (1789); second President of the United States.

Aaron Burr, New Jersey, was Jefferson's Vice President (1801), an able but disturbed politician, whose duel with Hamilton, and sad decline ruined his place in history.

Thomas Jefferson, Virginia, presided over the Senate (1797) as Vice President, under John Adams, and was elected third President of the United State.

Elbridge Gerry, Massachusetts, was Vice President (1813) under James Madison. A signer of the Declaration of Independence, later elected Governor of Massachusetts.

George Clinton, New York, Vice President (1805) in Jefferson's second term (an uncle of the better known De Witt Clinton), a member of the Continental Congress in 1775–76; served also as Vice President under James Madison.

Daniel D. Tompkins, New York, Vice President (1817) under James Monroe, Tompkins was Governor of New York and one of the founders of the New York Historical Society; re-elected with Monroe in 1820.

John C. Calhoun, South Carolina, Vice President (1825) under John Q. Adams. One of the south's great statesmen. Re-elected Vice President 1828 on the Jackson ticket.

Martin Van Buren, New York, was Vice President in the Jackson administration (1833) when Calhoun resigned on his election to the Senate. Succeeded to Presidency 1837.

Richard M. Johnson, Kentucky, Van Buren's Vice President (1837), soldier and Senator, voted into Vice Presidency by the Senate, because regular candidates failed of majority of electoral votes.

John Tyler, Virginia, Harrison's Vice President (1841), Representative and Senator, Governor, succeeded to Presidency on Harrison's death, was subject of the spirited campaign slogan: Tippecanoe and Tyler, too.

George M. Dallas, Pennsylvania, James K. Polk's Vice President (1845), Van Buren's Minister to Russia; President Pierce's Minister to Great Britain; one-time Mayor of Philadelphia.

Millard Fillmore, New York, Zachary Taylor's Vice President (1849) succeding him to the Presidency when Taylor died, fought in the Civil War on Union side, prominent in state and national politics.

William R. King, North Carolina, Franklin Pierce's Vice President (1853), was a Senator from Alabama, after having served as Representative from North Carolina. He also served as President pro tempore of the Senate.

John C. Breckinridge, Kentucky, James Buchanan's Vice President (1857) in the controversial era before Civil War—youngest Vice President up to that time, defeated for Presidency by Lincoln.

Hannibal Hamlin, Maine, Abraham Lincoln's Vice President (1861) was Speaker of the State House of Representatives; Senator, Governor of Maine, later Minister to Spain.

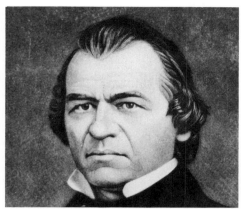

Andrew Johnson, North Carolina, and Tennessee, Lincoln's second-term Vice President (1865); totally self-educated; organized and led 1828 working-man's party; Governor of Tennessee and Senator; succeeded Lincoln on latter's death; acquitted of impeachment charges.

Schuyler Colfax, New York and Indiana, Grant's Vice President (1869); Speaker of House in 38th, 39th and 40th Congresses. Distinguished editor. Completely vindicated of corruption charges in 1873 Credit Mobilier scandal.

Henry Wilson, New Hampshire and Massachusetts; U.S. Grant's Vice President, succeeding Colfax (1873), owner-editor *Boston Republican,* active in Free Soil politics; Senator; died in Capitol, 1875.

William A. Wheeler, New York, Rutherford B. Hayes' Vice President (1877); elected Representative (Republican) to Thirty-Seventh, Forty-First, and three succeeding Congresses, then to Vice-Presidency.

Chester A. Arthur, Vermont and New York, James A. Garfield's Vice President (1881), succeeding to Presidency same year upon Garfield's assassination, held high military posts.

Thomas A. Hendricks, Ohio and Indiana, Grover Cleveland's Vice President (1885); Representative and Senator from Indiana; Governor of Indiana, 1872; failed Vice Presidential election with Tilden, 1876.

Levi P. Morton, Vermont and New York, Benjamin Harrison's Vice President (1889); Republican Representative to Forty-sixth and Forty-seventh Congresses; U.S. Minister to France 1881–85.

Adlai E. Stevenson, Kentucky and Illinois, grandfather of Democratic candidate for President, 1952 and 1956. He was Grover Cleveland's Vice President (1893) and a Member of Congress.

Garret A. Hobart, New Jersey, William McKinley's Vice President (1897), held state elective offices, including speakership of New Jersey Assembly. Died 1899 before end of Vice Presidential term.

Theodore Roosevelt, New York, William McKinley's Vice President (1901). Spanish-American war hero. Assistant Secretary of Navy; Governor of New York; President of the United States.

Charles W. Fairbanks, Ohio and Indiana, Theodore Roosevelt's Vice President (1905); Senator; resigned senatorship to run for Vice President with Roosevelt 1904; failed to be re-elected (with Hughes) 1916.

James S. Sherman, New York, William H. Taft's Vice President (1909); Mayor of Utica; Republican representative in Congress; renominated for Vice President in 1912 but died same year.

Thomas R. Marshall, Indiana, Woodrow Wilson's Vice President (1913); Governor of Indiana, 1909–13 re-elected Vice President, 1916; 1912 was choice of Indiana Democratic delegation for Presidency.

Calvin Coolidge, Vermont and Massachusetts; Warren G. Harding's Vice President (1921); Massachusetts Governor 1919–20, succeeded to Presidency 1921.

Charles G. Dawes, Ohio and Illinois; Calvin Coolidge's Vice President (1925); held high posts in World War I; utilities and banking executive; lawyer; first director Bureau of Budget.

Charles Curtis, Kansas; Herbert C. Hoover's Vice President (1929); Republican Representative and Senator; President pro tempore Senate December 4–12, 1911, Republican whip of Senate, 1915–24.

John Nance Garner, Texas; Franklin Delano Roosevelt's Vice President (1933); Representative to Congress and Judge; Minority Leader and Speaker of House; re-elected Vice President 1936.

Henry A. Wallace, Iowa; FDR's Vice President (1941); Editor, successful agricultural experimentalist; Secretary of Agriculture, 1933; Secretary of Commerce, 1945–46.

Harry S. Truman, Missouri, FDR's Vice President (1945); Lieutenant, Captain and Major, in World War I; Judge; elected U.S. Senate, 1934; re-elected, 1940; succeeded to Presidency.

Alben W. Barkley, Kentucky; Truman's Vice President (1949); Judge; temporary Chairman, democratic National Conventions, 1932 and 1936; permanent, 1940. Representative to Congress seven terms; elected U.S. Senate four times; Majority and Minority Leader.

Gerald R. Ford, Michigan. Richard Nixon's Vice President from December 6, 1973, until he became President of the United States on August 9, 1974. Former Representative from Michigan (1949–73) and House Minority Leader (1965–1973).

Richard Nixon, California; Dwight D. Eisenhower's Vice President (1953); Representative and Senator; Lieutenant-Commander World World War II; re-elected Vice-President, 1956; and elected President of U.S. in 1968 and 1972.

Lyndon B. Johnson, Texas; John F. Kennedy's Vice President (1961); Representative and Senator; public school teacher; Lieutenant-Commander World War II; Senate majority leader; President.

Hubert H. Humphrey, South Dakota and Minnesota; Johnson's Vice President (1965); pharmacist; instructor, political science, University of Louisiana and University of Minnesota; Minneapolis Mayor; elected Senate, 1948, 1954, 1960, and 1970.

Spiro T. Agnew, Maryland; Richard M. Nixon's Vice President (1969, until resignation, October 10, 1973); Governor of Maryland, 1967–69.

Nelson A. Rockefeller. Former Governor of New York (1959–1973), Nelson A. Rockefeller was inaugurated as the 41st Vice President of the United States and President of the Senate on December 19, 1974, before a live television audience, marking the first time the Senate permitted television cameras. He served until January 20, 1977.

Your Congress at Work

East Front, The Capitol

96th Congress Profile

Members of Congress are as diverse as the States and districts they represent. They reflect the pluralistic nature of our society.

The "typical" Member of Congress is sometimes alluded to, but such a portrait gives a distorted view. The Congress is composed of five hundred and thirty-nine individuals from our 50 States, and the District of Columbia and Puerto Rico, Guam and the Virgin Islands, and each Member has a different personal history. Yet, as is true of the American people, Members of Congress share many traits, as this following summary indicates.

Age

When the 96th Congress convened in January 1979, the average age of its Members was 49.5, the youngest in at least 30 years. The average age of Members of the House of Representatives was 48.8, making it the youngest House since at least the 60th Congress (1907–1909). The average age of Members of the Senate was 52.7, making it the youngest Senate since at least the 45th Congress (1877–1879).

The youngest Representative is freshman James Shannon, Democrat of Massachusetts, who is 27. The oldest Representative is Claude Pepper, Democrat of Florida, who is 79. Representatives must be at least 25 when they take office.

The youngest Senator is freshman Bill Bradley, Democrat of New Jersey, who is 36. The oldest Senator is Milton Young, Republican of North Dakota, who is 82. Senators must be at least 30 when they take office.

Father in the Senate, Son in the House. The only father and son combination serving together in the Congress, Senator Barry M. Goldwater of Arizona and Representative Barry M. Goldwater, Jr., of California.

Occupations

As has been true in most previous Congresses, law is the dominant profession of the Members of the 96th Congress. There are 270 lawyers. In addition, there are 156 Members with a business or banking background; 64 educators; 25 Members with a farming background; 11 with a journalism background; seven clergymen; six doctors, including a Senator who is a veterinarian and the delegate from the Virgin Islands who is a cardiologist; four scientists; and three engineers. In addition, there are at least 40 Members who are former congressional staffers; two Senators who are former astronauts; one Representative who is a pharmacist; and another two who are optometrists.

Representatives Phillip M. Crane, left and Daniel B. Crane of Illinois one of the two sets of brothers in the Congress.

Religion

During the last decade, the number of Members of Congress identifying with one religious denomination or another has remained over 90 percent. More than 500 of the Members of the 96th Congress cite a specific religious affiliation.

Although Protestants of various denominations collectively hold more seats in the 96th Congress, Roman Catholics, with 129 in the two Houses, make up the largest contingent of any one denomination. Of the Protestants, there are 77 Methodists, 68 Episcopalians, 64 Presbyterians, 54 Baptists, and 20 Lutherans. There are also 30 Jewish Members of Congress and smaller numbers of members of numerous other religious groups.

Education

The Members of the 96th Congress are highly educated. There are at least 332 Representatives and 80 Senators with bachelors degrees; 67 Representatives and 15 Senators with masters degrees; 196 Representatives and 60 Senators with law degrees; four Representatives, one Delegate, and one Senator with medical degrees; and 16 Representatives and four Senators with Doctoral degrees.

Congressional Service

The average length of service of Representatives in the 96th Congress is 7.79 years or almost four terms. Representatives are elected for two-year terms. Representative Jamie Whitten, Democrat of Mississippi, has served longer in the House than any other Member of the 96th Congress. He is the Dean of the House and his service began on November 4, 1941.

Representative Claude Pepper of Florida. The only incumbent Member of Congress to have first served in the Senate and then the House.

The average length of service of Senators in the 96th Congress is 8.60 years or slightly more than one and one-third term. Senators are elected for six-year terms. Senator Warren Magnuson, Democrat of Washington, has served longer in the Senate than any other Member of the 96th Congress. He is the President Pro Tempore of the Senate and his service began on December 14, 1944.

Sex and Race

There are 17 women serving in the 96th Congress, one Senator and 16 Representatives. This number is less than the number of women who served in the 94th and 95th Congresses when there were 19 and 20 women respectively.

There are 17 black Members of the 96th Congress, all serving in the House of Representatives. This is one less than the number who served in the 95th Congress when there were 18 black Members including one black Senator. There are currently 6 Hispanic Members and 6 Members with an Oriental heritage.

Brothers, Representatives Phillip M. Burton, left and John L. Burton of California.

Women in American Politics

Jeannette Rankin of Montana became the first woman to serve in the United States Congress when she was elected to the House of Representatives to serve in the 65th Congress (1917–1919) as her State's Representative-At-Large. Since that time, 102 other women have been elected or appointed to Congress. Ninety have served in the House of Representatives, including one delegate from Hawaii; and 14 have served in the Senate. Margaret Chase Smith of Maine is the only woman to have served in both Houses. She served in the House from June 10, 1940, until January 3, 1949, when she began her Senate service. When she left the Senate on January 3, 1973, she had served longer there than any other woman, a distinction she still holds.

Until the election of Nancy Landon Kassebaum of Kansas to the 96th Congress, all of the women Senators had first been elected or appointed to Congress to fill unexpired terms of Senators who had resigned or died in office. Seven of them were elected or appointed to complete the terms of their husbands who died while serving. Senator Kassebaum is the first woman elected to the Senate without having first filled an unexpired term; and she is one of only four women who were ever elected to full six-year terms in the Senate. The others were Hattie W. Caraway of Arkansas, Maurine C. Neuberger of Oregon, and Margaret Chase Smith.

Of the women who have served in the House of Representatives, 34 have been elected to fill vacancies caused by death or resignation of a Member. Twenty-eight, including two in the 96th Congress, were first elected to fill the terms of their late husbands; and

Jeannette Rankin, an ardent suffragette, was elected to the 65th Congress in 1916, becoming the first woman Member of the House; and was elected again to the 77th Congress in 1941. Ironically, during her two separate terms, Congress declared war (1917 and 1941) and thus she became the only Representative to vote against both declarations.

Congresswoman's Suite which is located in the Capitol was at one time used as the Speaker's Office. John Quincy Adams, the sixth President of the United States died in this room in 1848. Pictured (R. to L.) are Representatives Gladys Spellman (Maryland); Marilyn Lloyd Bouquard (Tennessee); Beverly B. Byron (Maryland); Marjorie S. Holt (Maryland); Patricia Schroeder (Colorado); Margaret N. Heckler (Massachusetts); Geraldine Ann Ferraro (New York); Shirley Chisholm (New York); Virginia Smith (Nebraska)

(left to right) Cardiss Collins of Illinois, Olympia J. Snowe of Maine, Corinne C. (Lindy) Boggs of Lousiana, standing (left to right) Elizabeth Holtzman of New York, Barbara A. Mikulski of Maryland and Mary Rose Oakar of Ohio.

Suffragettes picket White House. This passive scene, in January 1917, illustrates women's early fight for political self-respect.

fourteen of these were subsequently reelected to their own terms. Another woman, a Member of the 96th Congress, ran for office after the death of her husband who was serving in the 95th Congress and died prior to the election of the 96th Congress. Winnifred Mason Huck of Illinois was elected to the 67th Congress (1921–1923) to complete the term of her father who died in office.

Edith Nourse Rogers of Massachusetts holds the record of longevity of service by women in the House. She was elected to fill the vacancy caused by the death of her husband and served from June 25, 1925, until her death on September 10, 1960.

Of the 44 women who first entered Congress before 1949, 57 percent were first elected to fill another Member's unexpired term, and 43 percent were elected in a general election. Of the 59 women who first entered Congress after January 1949, 36 percent were chosen to fill vacancies, and 64 percent were elected in the general election. Forty-one percent of the women elected before 1949 succeeded their husbands in office, while only 25 percent of the women entering Congress after 1949 succeeded their husbands.

The Sewall-Belmont House, home of the National Woman's Party, is located near the two newest Senate office buildings. It was declared a National Historic Site by act of Congress in 1975 in recognition of the women's suffrage movement.

During the War of 1812 the only shot fired against the British troops who burned the Capitol were fired from this house. Secretary of the Treasury Gallatin resided here during the development and signing of the Louisiana Purchase.

Visitors are welcome each weekday from 10:00 a.m. to 2:00 p.m. and noon to 4:00 p.m. Saturday and Sunday.

Thus, since 1949, most of the women in Congress have been elected on their own for a full term.

Jeannette Rankin, the first woman Member of Congress, was elected before the ratification of the Nineteenth Amendment in 1919 which gave suffrage to all female citizens of the United States. She served one term in the House, the 65th Congress (1917–1919), during which she campaigned unsuccessfully for election to the Senate in the 66th Congress. However, she was reelected to the House in 1940 and served in the 77th Congress (1941–1943). Ms. Rankin is the only Member of Congress to have opposed America's entry into both World Wars. In 1917, she joined with her male colleagues in voting against American participation in World War I; and during her second term in 1941, she was the only Member of Congress to oppose passage of the American declaration of war against Japan after the attack on Pearl Harbor.

Of the 14 women who have served in the Senate, Rebecca Felton of Georgia, who was appointed to the 67th Congress in 1922, holds at least two Senate records. She was the first female Senator; and at age 87, she was the oldest person ever to begin Senate service. Hattie Caraway of Arkansas was the first woman elected to a full six-year Senate term. She was appointed to the Senate in November 1931 to fill the vacancy caused by the death of her husband, and elected in January 1932 to fill the remainder of his term. She was reelected in 1938 and completed her service on January 3, 1945.

Representative Shirley Chisholm of New York is the first black woman to serve in Congress. She was first elected to the 91st Congress (1969–1971), and has been reelected ever since. Three other black women have been elected to Congress, all to the House of Representatives. They are Cardiss Collins of Illinois, the present head of the Congressional Black Caucus, who began her service in the 93d Congress; and Barbara Jordan of Texas and Yvonne Burke of California, both of whom served in the 93d, 94th, and 95th Congresses. Representative Burke also was the first and only Member of Congress to give birth while in office. Her daughter was born during the 93d Congress.

To date, seven women have chaired congressional committees. As head of the House Committee on Expenditures in the Post Office Department in the 68th Congress (1923–1925), Mae Ella Nolan of California was the first. Hattie Caraway of Arkansas is the only woman to have chaired a Senate committee. She was head of the Committee on Enrolled Bills from the 73d through the 78th Congresses. Other women have chaired the following committees of the House of Representatives: District of Columbia Committee; House Administration Committee; Labor Committee; Committee on the Election of the President, Vice President, and Members of Congress; Veterans' Affairs Committee; and the Merchant Marine and Fisheries Committee.

There are 17 women currently serving in the 96th Congress, one Senator and 16 Representatives. Twenty is the largest number of women to serve in Congress at the same time, and this occurred in the 87th and 95th Congresses. Nineteen is the largest number of women to serve in the House at the same time. There were 19 women Representatives in the 94th Congress. Three is the largest number of women to serve in the Senate at the same time; there were three female Senators in both the 75th and 83d Congresses.

Memorial to the Pioneers of the Women's Suffrage Movement.

This portrait monument of Elizabeth Cady Stanton, Susan B. Anthony and Lucretia Mott was accepted as a gift from the women of the United States, through the National Woman's Party, by the Joint Committee on the Library, February 15, 1921. The original block of marble from which these busts were carved measured 7'x5'8''x5', and the estimated weight is between 7 and 8 tons.

In accepting the monument the Joint Committee on the Library directed that it be placed temporarily "in the Rotunda for the purpose of appropriate ceremonies of tender and reception and at the conclusion of the ceremonies, the said sculpture be placed in the Crypt on the first floor of the Capitol beneath the Dome." It was moved from the Rotunda to the Crypt May 1921.

Elected in 1978, Senator Nancy Landon Kassebaum (R-Kansas) is the first woman elected to the United States Senate without having been preceded in office by a spouse or appointed to fill an unexpired term. She is the daughter of Alfred M. Landon, 1936 Republican presidential nominee and former Kansas Governor.

Your Member Represents You

Representative Ronald V. Dellums of California, left, and Representative Cardiss Collins of Illinois meet with Alex Haley author of *Roots* during his recent visit to the Capitol.

Speaker Thomas P. O'Neill, Jr., of Massachusetts greets the March of Dimes Poster Child in his Capitol office.

Senator Mark O. Hatfield of Oregon greets a friend and constituent from Oregon.

Senator Lloyd Bentsen of Texas (left), greets a member of the shrimp industry at a Washington reception.

Representative Ron Marlenee of Montana meets in his Capitol office farmers during the recent agriculture strike.

Representative Mary Rose Oakar of Ohio greets a group of Cub and Boy Scouts and Girl Scouts.

Senator Spark M. Matsunaga of Hawaii during a recent tour of the Capitol with some of his constituents from the state of Hawaii.

Senator Daniel K. Inouye of Hawaii talks with a group of students during one of his visits to the University of Hawaii campus in Honolulu.

Representative Margaret M. Heckler of Massachusetts (center), receives a momento from two 4-H Ambassadors.

Senator Howard M. Metzenbaum of Ohio greets a group of young students during their tour to the Capitol.

Senator Henry M. Jackson of Washington talks with students participating in a Presidential classroom in Washington.

Senator John Melcher of Montana talks to a group from Montana on their recent visit to Washington.

Senator Claiborne Pell of Rhode Island greets a family from Rhode Island in his Capitol office.

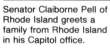

Representative John J. Duncan of Tennessee with supporters from the State of Tennessee.

Representative Beryl Anthony, Jr. of Arkansas meets with a family from his district.

Representative Mike McCormick of Washington inspects an experimental electric vehicle on the East front of the Capitol.

Representative G. V. (Sonny) Montgomery greets a group of constituents from his district in Mississippi on the Capitol steps.

Representative Michael Barnes of Maryland holds a group discussion with a group of students from Maryland.

Representative Robert E. Bauman of Maryland greets a group of students from his district.

Representative Tom Foley of Washington (right), meets with Kirk O'Donnell, General Counsel to the Speaker, and Mary McGrory of the Washington Star.

Representative Claude Pepper of Florida in his Capitol office with a group of summer interns.

Representative Donald Joseph Albosta of Michigan discusses farm legislation with a group of farmers from his district.

Senator Howard Baker, Jr. of Tennessee is questioned on the Senate steps by Phil Jones of CBS News.

Representative Augustus F. Hawkins of California greets a group of constituents in his office.

Senator Jacob K. Javits of New York in his Hill office with students from New York.

Mrs. Averell Harriman welcomes Senator George McGovern of South Dakota, to a reception for Democratic leaders.

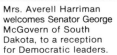

Representative John J. Cavanaugh of Nebraska with his son and daughter at the Congressional swearing-in ceremonies.

Representative Norman D. Dicks of Washington welcomes some of his young constituents.

Senator Robert Morgan of North Carolina, center, chatting with Colonel Sanders and a member of the Colonel's staff at a luncheon in the Capitol.

Representative Tom Steed of Oklahoma greets a group of students from Oklahoma on their recent tour to Washington.

Representative Gladys Noon Spellman of Maryland, third from right, meets with a group of constituents in her Hill office.

Representative Daniel K. Akaka of Hawaii with constituents from Hawaii.

Senator Howard W. Cannon of Nevada, right, testifies before a Senate committee on behalf of a Nevada constituent.

Representative William L. Dickinson of Alabama, addressing thousands of farmers who came to Washington.

Representative Dave Stockman of Michigan meets with two constituents in his mobile office.

A Montana 4-H group visits Senator Max Baucus (far left—top row) and Representative Pat Williams (center—top row) on their visit to Washington.

Representative Floyd Spence of South Carolina meets a group of students from South Carolina.

Representative Henry B. Gonzalez of Texas and his friend on the Capitol steps.

A student participating in Girl's Nation meets with Senator Bob Packwood of Oregon in his office.

Representative Barbara A. Mikulski of Maryland (second from right—front row), welcomes friends from her district to the Capitol.

Representative Jack Brooks of Texas explains the workings of Congress to his summer interns.

Representative John Joseph Moakley (far right) greets some of his constituents from Massachusetts.

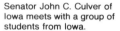

Senator John Tower of Texas (center), at a Washington reception for Texans.

Senator John C. Culver of Iowa meets with a group of students from Iowa.

Philadelphia students visit with Representative Raymond F. Lederer.

Representative Edward P. Boland of Massachusetts meets with a group of constituents during their recent visit to the Capitol.

APATHY? Representative James C. Cleveland of New Hampshire struggles valiantly to arouse some interest in his legislation from an otherwise engaged young constituent.

Students from Rockhurst College in Kansas City, Missouri, meet with their Representative in Congress, Richard Bolling, in his Washington office to discuss the legislative process.

The Committee System / Congress at Work

Members of the Senate
Foreign Relations
Committee (right to left),
Senators George S.
McGovern of South
Dakota; Claiborne Pell of
Rhode Island; Chairman
Frank Church of Idaho;
Jacob K. Javits of New
York; Charles H. Percy of
Illinois and Howard H.
Baker, Jr. of Tennessee.

Congress in its committee rooms is Congress at work, wrote Woodrow Wilson. It is in the committees of Congress that bills undergo their closest scrutiny, that investigations—including oversight of the executive branch—are conducted, and that the differences in bills passed by each House are reconciled into one version acceptable to both.

Congress uses four different types of committees to perform these different functions: standing committees, select or special committees, joint committees and conference committees.

Committees that continue from Congress to Congress are called *standing committees.* The subject jurisdictions of these permanent committees are set forth in the Rules of each House, and virtually every introduced bill is referred to one or more of them according to the subjects involved. These are the committees that actually review proposed legislation and determine which bills shall be reported to each House.

Mrs. Rosalynn Carter
testifies before the House
Select Committee on
Aging.

Representative Adam
Benjamin, Jr., of Indiana,
Chairman, House
Appropriations
Subcommittee on
Legislative Branch confers
with staff member prior to
hearing.

Speaker Thomas P.
O'Neill, Jr., of
Massachusetts appears
before a House Committee
to testify in favor of
legislation for emergency
fuel assistance for welfare
recipients.

In the 96th Congress, there are 22 standing committees in the House and 15 in the Senate. Most have several subcommittees with specific jurisdictions. Usually a standing committee sends a bill to one of its subcommittees for hearings, review, and recommendations. The bill is then reported to the full committee for consideration. Finally, if approved by the full committee, the bill is reported to the full House or Senate.

Standing committees are also responsible for overseeing the operations of the executive departments and agencies under their respective jurisdictions. They usually perform this function by studies which provide Congress with the facts necessary to determine whether the agencies are administering legislation as intended. Congressional studies also help committees identify areas in which legislative action might be needed and the form that action might take.

Other Congressional studies are performed by *select* or *special committees.* Usually established for a limited period of time, these groups ordinarily deal with more specific subjects and issues than do the standing committees. For example, in recent years each House has established a select committee on aging to study the multitude of problems that affect senior citizens.

Senator Robert Morgan of North Carolina (left) receives some material from Senator Lawton Chiles of Florida (far right) prior to a meeting of the Senate Intelligence Committee. In the middle is Senator Barry Goldwater of Arizona.

Members of the Senate Rules and Administration Committee (left to right), Senators Mark O. Hatfield of Oregon, Ranking Minority Member; Chairman Claiborne Pell of Rhode Island; Howard W. Cannon of Nevada and Majority Leader Robert C. Byrd of West Virginia during a committee hearing.

Former Secretary of State Henry Kissinger testifies before the Senate Foreign Relations Committee.

Representative Barbara Mikulski of Maryland chairs a meeting of the House Subcommittee on Transportation and Commerce.

Members of the Senate Governmental Operations Committee listen to a witness during a recent hearing (right to left), Chairman Abraham Ribicoff of Connecticut; Senator Charles H. Percy of Illinois, Ranking Minority Member; Senator William V. Roth of Delaware and Senator Jacob K. Javits of New York.

Prior to testifying before the House Committee on the Judiciary, Former President Gerald R. Ford confers with Committee Chairman Peter W. Rodino of New Jersey (second from right); Representative Jack Brooks of Texas (right), and Representative Tom Railsback of Illinois.

Select committees in one House or the other have also studied population problems, narcotics, and Indian affairs. During the past decade, each House has used a select committee to study its own committee system and to recommend improvements. Most select committees may investigate, study, and make recommendations but may not report legislation. But both Houses have created a few permanent select committees in recent years and authorized them to report legislation.

Congress uses *joint committees* for investigatory and housekeeping purposes. These are usually permanent bodies composed of an equal number of House and Senate Members. Although in the past certain joint committees had the authority to consider and report legislation, no joint committee had that power in the 96th Congress. Usually joint committees are used to study broad and complex areas over a long period of time, an example being the Joint Economic Committee. Other joint committees, such as the Joint Committee on Printing, oversee functions connected with the operation of the legislative branch.

The last category of committee is the *conference committee*. These are formed to reconcile the differences between the House and Senate when each passes a different version of the same bill. Conference committees are ad hoc joint committees, temporary panels appointed to deal with a single piece of legislation, dissolving upon the completion of that task. Members of both Houses serve on each conference committee, and the number of Members from each House may be the same. This is not as inequitable as it might seem because the voting in conference committees is by House; its decisions must be approved by a majority of the Representatives and a majority of the Senators on the committee.

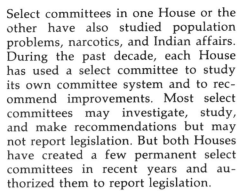

Chairman Richard Bolling of Missouri, far left-top row, Chairs meeting of House Rules Committee.

Four Senators hold a joint hearing on a mutual issue concerning their States. (left to right) Senators Jesse A. Helms of North Carolina; William Proxmire of Wisconsin; Harrison A. Williams of New Jersey and Robert Morgan of North Carolina.

Representatives Jerry M. Patterson of California, left, Chairman, and James C. Cleveland of New Hampshire, Ranking Minority Member of the House Select Committee on Committees review hearing agenda.

Senators Edward M. Kennedy of Massachusetts and George McGovern of South Dakota meet the press after a committee hearing.

Representatives Louis Stokes of Cleveland, left, past chairman, former Select Committee on Assassinations and Samuel L. Devine, ranking minority Member during hearings.

Every Member of the House must serve on at least one standing committee except the Speaker and minority leader who, by tradition, serve on none. Senators *must* serve on at least two standing committees. Counting standing, select, and joint committee assignments, some Senators sit on as many as five or six. In the House approximately 90 Representatives have only one committee assignment, usually because they sit on a particularly busy panel like Appropriations. All other House Members sit on two or three committees. In one way or another, both Houses limit the number of chairmanships any single Member may hold.

Committee sizes vary considerably and sometimes change from Congress to Congress. Because the House has more than four times as many Members as the Senate, its committees are generally larger. In the 96th Congress, the largest House committee—Appropriations—had 54 members, the largest Senate committee—also Appropriations—had 28. Most Senate standing committees have from 14 to 20 members, most House committees from 30 to 45. Traditionally, party ratios on committees correspond roughly to the party ratio in the full Chamber.

Committee and subcommittee service encourages Members to specialize in the subject areas of the panels on which they sit. Thus, the committee system continually builds up a reservoir of expertise to guide Congress as it attempts to deal with the Nation's problems.

Senator Henry M. Jackson of Washington (left), Chairman of the Senate Energy and Natural Resources Committee, Representative Harley O. Staggers of West Virginia (center), Chairman, House Interstate and Foreign Commerce Committee and Senator Spark M. Matsunaga of Hawaii a Member of the Senate Energy and Natural Resources Committee during a break of a recent House-Senate Energy Conference.

Chairman John Joseph Moakley of Massachusetts, right, of the Subcommittee on Rules of the House confers with Representative Butler Derrick of South Carolina.

Members of the House Committee on Education and Labor (left to right), Representatives William F. Goodling of Pennsylvania, Chairman Carl D. Perkins of Kentucky, Ted Weiss of New York and Ray Kogovsek of Colorado during a recent hearing.

Representative Frank Thompson, Jr., of New Jersey, center, Chairman, Committee on House Administration presides during committee meeting.

Standing Committees of the United States Senate

Armed Services

Chairman,
John C. Stennis
Mississippi

Ranking Minority Member
John Tower
Texas

Agriculture, Nutrition, and Forestry

Chairman,
Herman E. Talmadge
Georgia

Ranking Minority Member
Jesse Helms
North Carolina

Banking, Housing, and Urban Affairs

Chairman,
William Proxmire
Wisconsin

Ranking Minority Member
Jake Garn
Utah

Appropriations

Chairman,
Warren G. Magnuson
Washington

Ranking Minority Member
Milton R. Young
North Dakota

Budget

Chairman,
Edmund S. Muskie
Maine

Ranking Minority Member
Henry Bellmon
Oklahoma

Commerce, Science, and Transportation

Chairman,
Howard W. Cannon
Nevada

Ranking Minority Member
Bob Packwood
Oregon

Foreign Relations

Chairman,
Frank Church
Idaho

Ranking Minority Member
Jacob K. Javits
New York

Rules and Administration

Chairman,
Claiborne Pell
Rhode Island

Ranking Minority Member
Mark O. Hatfield
Oregon

Energy and Natural Resources

Chairman,
Henry M. Jackson
Washington

Ranking Minority Member
Mark O. Hatfield
Oregon

Governmental Affairs

Chairman,
Abraham Ribicoff
Connecticut

Ranking Minority Member
Charles H. Percy
Illinois

Veterans' Affairs

Chairman,
Alan Cranston
California

Ranking Minority Member
Alan K. Simpson
Wyoming

Environment and Public Works

Chairman,
Jennings Randolph
West Virginia

Ranking Minority Member
Robert T. Stafford
Vermont

Judiciary

Chairman,
Edward M. Kennedy
Massachusetts

Ranking Minority Member
Strom Thurmond
South Carolina

Finance

Chairman,
Russell B. Long
Louisiana

Ranking Minority Member
Bob Dole
Kansas

Labor and Human Resources

Chairman,
Harrison A. Williams, Jr.
New Jersey

Ranking Minority Member
Richard S. Schweiker
Pennsylvania

Select and Special Committees of the United States Senate

Ethics

Chairman,
Howell Heflin
Alabama

Vice Chairman,
Malcolm Wallop
Wyoming

Intelligence

Chairman,
Birch Bayh
Indiana

Ranking Minority Member
Barry Goldwater
Arizona

Aging

Chairman,
Lawton Chiles
Florida

Ranking Minority Member
Pete V. Domenici
New Mexico

Indian Affairs

Chairman,
John Melcher
Montana

Ranking Minority Member
William S. Cohen
Maine

Small Business

Chairman,
Gaylord Nelson
Wisconsin

Ranking Minority Member
Lowell P. Weicker, Jr.
Connecticut

Standing Committees of the United States House of Representatives

Appropriations

Chairman,
Jamie L. Whitten
Mississippi

Ranking Minority Member
Silvio O. Conte
Massachusetts

Banking, Finance and Urban Affairs

Chairman,
Henry S. Reuss
Wisconsin

Ranking Minority Member
J. William Stanton
Ohio

Agriculture

Chairman,
Thomas S. Foley
Washington

Ranking Minority Member
William C. Wampler
Virginia

Armed Services

Chairman,
Melvin Price
Illinois

Ranking Minority Member
Bob Wilson
California

Budget

Chairman,
Robert N. Giaimo
Connecticut

Ranking Minority Member
Delbert L. Latta
Ohio

District of Columbia

Chairman,
Ronald V. Dellums
California

Ranking Minority Member
Stewart B. McKinney
Connecticut

House Administration

Chairman,
Frank Thompson, Jr.
New Jersey

Ranking Minority Member
William L. Dickinson
Alabama

Merchant Marine and Fisheries

Chairman,
John M. Murphy
New York

Ranking Minority Member
Paul N. McCloskey, Jr.
California

Education and Labor

Chairman,
Carl D. Perkins
Kentucky

Ranking Minority Member
John M. Ashbrook
Ohio

Interior and Insular Affairs

Chairman,
Morris K. Udall
Arizona

Ranking Minority Member
Don H. Clausen
California

Post Office and Civil Service

Chairman,
James M. Hanley
New York

Ranking Minority Member
Edward J. Derwinski
Illinois

Foreign Affairs

Chairman,
Clement J. Zablocki
Wisconsin

Ranking Minority Member
William S. Broomfield
Michigan

Interstate and Foreign Commerce

Chairman,
Harley O. Staggers
West Virginia

Ranking Minority Member
James T. Broyhill
North Carolina

Public Works and Transportation

Chairman,
Harold T. Johnson
California

Ranking Minority Member
William H. Harsha
Ohio

Government Operations

Chairman,
Jack Brooks
Texas

Ranking Minority Member
Frank Horton
New York

Judiciary

Chairman,
Peter W. Rodino, Jr.
New Jersey

Ranking Minority Member
Robert McClory
Illinois

Rules

Chairman,
Richard Bolling
Missouri

Ranking Minority Member
James H. Quillen
Tennessee

Standing Committees
of the United States
House of Representatives
—continued

Small Business

Chairman,
Neal Smith
Iowa

Ranking Minority Member
Joseph M. McDade
Pennsylvania

Veterans' Affairs

Chairman,
Ray Roberts
Texas

Ranking Minority Member
John Paul
Hammerschmidt
Arkansas

Science and Technology

Chairman,
Don Fuqua
Florida

Ranking Minority Member
John W. Wydler
New York

Standards of Official Conduct

Chairman,
Charles E. Bennett
Florida

Ranking Minority Member
Floyd Spence
South Carolina

Ways and Means

Chairman,
Al Ullman
Oregon

Ranking Minority Member
Barber B. Conable, Jr.
New York

Select and Special
Committees of
the United States
House of Representatives

Committee on Committees

Chairman,
Jerry M. Patterson
California

Ranking Minority Member
James C. Cleveland
New Hampshire

Narcotics Abuse and Control

Chairman,
Lester L. Wolff
New York

Ranking Minority Member
Tom Railsback
Illinois

Aging

Chairman,
Claude Pepper
Florida

Ranking Minority Member
Charles E. Grassley
Iowa

Intelligence

Chairman,
Edward P. Boland
Massachusetts

Ranking Minority Member
J. Kenneth Robinson
Virginia

Outer Continental Shelf

Chairman,
John M. Murphy
New York

Ranking Minority Member
Edwin B. Forsythe
New Jersey

Joint Committees of the United States Congress

Library

Chairman
Senator Claiborne Pell
Rhode Island

Vice Chairman
Representative Lucien N. Nedzi
Michigan

Taxation

Chairman
Representative Al Ullman
Oregon

Vice Chairman
Senator Russell B. Long
Louisiana

Economic

Chairman
Senator Lloyd M. Bentsen
Texas

Vice Chairman
Representative Richard Bolling
Missouri

Printing

Chairman
Representative Frank Thompson, Jr.
New Jersey

Vice Chairman
Senator Claiborne Pell
Rhode Island

Two Committee Rooms of the Congress.

Revenue and Appropriations

"The Congress Shall Have Power to Lay and Collect Taxes, . . ."
(Sec. 8, Art. 1)

Collecting and spending money are basic and crucial governmental powers. Under our Constitution the executive branch carries out these responsibilities, but within limits established by Congress.

The government collects its revenues through taxes, excises, duties, customs and the sale of bonds, among other means. These monies pay for the operation of the Federal government and the financing of Federal programs.

Article I, Section 8, of the Constitution declares that "The Congress shall have the Power to lay and collect Taxes, Duties, Imposts, and Excises, to pay the Debts and provide for the common Defense and general Welfare of the United States . . . " Thus, the Congress, not the President, is empowered to impose taxes. When the Founding Fathers wrote this section of the Constitution, the memory of outrageous actions by colonial Governors was still fresh in their minds. They

Senator Warren G. Magnuson of Washington, left, Chairman, and Senator Milton R. Young of North Dakota, Ranking Minority Member, Senate Appropriations Committee meet in the beautiful committee room located in S–128 of the Capitol.

were determined to prevent the Executive from laying arbitrary taxes on the people. Thus, Article I, Section 7, of the Constitution further states that "All Bills for raising Revenue shall originate in the House of Representatives; but the Senate may propose or concur with Amendments as on other Bills."

Under their respective rules, the responsibility for drafting tax laws lies with the Ways and Means Committee in the House and the Finance Committee in the Senate. Because their decisions directly and significantly affect the nation's economy and the lives of virtually all Americans, these two committees are considered to be among the most powerful in Congress.

Federal agencies and departments spend money under the terms of appropriation laws enacted by Congress. These laws specify how much may be spent for each government program and activity during a stated period of time, usually one year. As with revenue measures, the Constitution gives the appropriation powers to Congress. Article I, Section 9 states: "No money shall be drawn from the Treasury, but in Consequence of Appropriations made by Law; and a regular statement and account of receipts and expenditures of all public money shall be published from time to time." By loosening the government's purse strings or by pulling them tighter, Congress can compel executive agencies to increase or decrease their spending and thereby determine the scope of their activities.

Although the Constitution does not explicitly empower the House to initiate appropriation bills, the House does so by custom. The Senate, as with revenue and all other measures sent to it by the House, may amend appropriation bills, increasing or decreasing amounts and inserting items of appropriation on its own initiative.

The Appropriations Committees of each House are vested with primary responsibility for recommending spending amounts. Not surprisingly, these committees are also generally ranked among the most powerful in Congress.

Ways and Means Committee members (right to left) Representative Barber Conable of New York, Chairman Al Ullman of Oregon, and Representative Dan Rostenkowski of Illinois confer with staff prior to Committee meeting.

Senator Russell Long of Louisiana, right, Chairman of the Senate Finance Committee; Senator Abraham Ribicoff of Connecticut, center, and Senator Harry F. Byrd, Jr., of Virginia, left, listen to testimony at Senate Finance Committee meeting.

Revenue, appropriations and budget decisions made by these twelve Members of Congress and the six committees they lead touch the pocketbook of every American.

(Top, left to right.):

Representatives Jamie Whitten, Mississippi, Chairman of the House Appropriations Committee; Silvio Conte, Massachusetts, Ranking Minority Member; Senators Warren Magnuson, Washington, Chairman of the Senate Appropriations Committee; Milton Young, North Dakota, Ranking Minority Member.

Representatives Al Ullman, Oregon, Chairman of the Ways and Means Committee; Barber Conable, New York, Ranking Minority Member. Senators Russell Long, Louisiana, Chairman of the Senate Finance Committee; Robert Dole, Kansas, Ranking Minority Member.

Representatives Robert Giaimo, Connecticut, Chairman of House Committee on the Budget; Delbert Latta, Ohio, Ranking Minority Member; and Senators Edmund Muskie, Maine, Chairman of the Senate Budget Committee; and Henry Bellmon, Oklahoma, Ranking Minority Member.

Senator Edmund Muskie of Maine, center, Chairman of the Senate Budget Committee; Senator Henry Bellmon of Oklahoma, left; Ranking Minority Member and Senator Lawton Chiles of Florida, right, during a markup meeting of the Committee.

At one time, the revenue and appropriations committees made just about all the important decisions on raising and spending money. Today their decisions, although still crucial, are part of a complex budget process involving the legislative or authorizing committees as well as the executive branch.

Since 1921 the law has required the President to take the first step in this process: preparing and submitting to Congress in each January his budget recommendations for the entire government. Then Congress takes over.

It sends tax proposals to the revenue committees, spending proposals to the appropriations committees, and legislative proposals to the authorizing committees. Under the rules of both Houses, bills authorizing the existence of many government agencies and activities must be acted on before appropriations for them may be considered. Thus, the authorizing committees recommend policies and activities while the appropriations committees recommend spending amounts.

Until recently Congress had no mechanisms for considering the budget in an integrated way. Each committee focused solely on its parts of the budget and brought those parts to the floor of its House for separate action. Neither the Congress nor any of its committees ever put the parts together to consider the budget as a whole, to compare the total revenue and spending amounts, to calculate the resulting surplus or deficit, or to determine whether such a surplus or deficit was desirable. Nor did Congress or any of its committees ever consider overall spending priorities: what proportion of the government's resources should go to defense, to social programs, to agriculture, and so forth. By default, Congress left these concerns to the President.

Many Members of Congress, and others, believed that the legislature was evading its responsibilities by clinging to this approach. They argued that Congress, lacking the means for developing alternatives to the President's budget, was reduced to mere tinkering with its details.

Congress responded to these criticisms in 1974 by enacting the Congressional Budget and Impoundment Control Act. This Act created a Budget Committee in each House to examine the budget as a whole, to review spending priorities, and to suggest alternatives to the President's budget proposals. A non-partisan Congressional Budget Office was established to provide Congress with budetary information and analyses. A new procedure was set up to give Congress the opportunity to consider the budget as a whole, and a timetable was adopted to encourage the timely enactment of authorization and appropriation bills.

Under these new arrangements, each Budget Committee reviews the President's budget plus recommendations from all other committees early in the year. By April 15 the Budget Committees must report a concurrent resolution embodying their recommendations for overall budget amounts and for spending in all of the major functional categories. Congress is supposed to complete its consideration of this first budget resolution by May 15. The purpose of the first budget resolution is to set targets for Congress and its committees as the individual parts of the budget come up for consideration.

Between May and September Congress must enact all of its spending bills. By September 15 it must agree to a second concurrent budget resolution, also reported by the Budget Committees, setting the final budget figures. These figures in the second resolution are binding; bills that break the spending ceiling or revenue floor in that resolution are subject to points of order that prevent them from being considered.

The House Appropriations Committee for the 96th Congress.

House Committee on the Budget Members (left to right) Chairman Robert N. Giaimo of Connecticut, Ranking Minority Member Delbert Latta of Ohio and Representative Eldon Rudd of Arizona discuss legislation prior to Committee hearing.

Congress in International Affairs

Sir Winston Churchill, Prime Minister of Great Britain, addresses a Joint Meeting. May, 1943.

The expanded role of Congress in foreign affairs in the seventies has resulted in vastly increased contacts between the Congress and foreign dignitaries visiting the United States. The House Foreign Affairs and Senate Foreign Relations Committees have the responsibility for the reception of these dignitaries. For example, the House Foreign Affairs Committee has hosted 50 meetings with heads of state, foreign ministers, and with delegations from around the world, during the first six months of the 96th Congress alone.

Additionally Members of Congress meet annually with members of foreign legislatures to exchange information, opinions and knowledge and to promote closer relationships among parliamentary bodies in the free world.

The Congress of the United States is a leading and influential participant in these interparliamentary meetings, where discussions and policy resolutions are aimed at improving world amity, peace, and the free exchange of people and ideas.

The oldest formally organized interparliamentary body is the Interparliamentary Union, established in 1889, to which all nations claiming to have parliamentary forms of government may apply for membership. The total number of nations varies from year to year but averages about 75, including several of the Eastern bloc countries. The group meets twice annually, in the spring and in the fall, with each meeting held in a different country. The Chairman of the United States Delegation to the 1979 fall conference in Caracas, Venezuela was Representative Richardson Preyer of North Carolina who is President of the American Branch of the Interparliamentary Union for the 96th Congress.

The North Atlantic Treaty Organization Parliamentarians' Conference (later renamed the North Atlantic Assembly) was formed in 1955. United

As head of the minority party in Parliament, Margaret Thatcher exchanged visits with Senator Jesse Helms of North Carolina. In 1979, Margaret Thatcher became Prime Minister of Great Britain.

With the aid of interpreters Representative Jack Brooks of Texas confers with Vice Premier Deng Xiao Ping of the People's Republic of China.

States participation was authorized in Public Law 689, 84th Congress, 2d Session, approved on July 11, 1956.

The North Atlantic Assembly holds an annual plenary session each autumn in one of the NATO countries. Committees of the Assembly meet throughout the year.

Representative Phillip Burton of California has served since 1977 as Chairman of the U.S. House of Representatives Delegation to the Assembly. In 1978, the Chairman of the Senate Delegation was Senator Claiborne Pell of Rhode Island. Representative Jack Brooks is the U.S. member on the Standing Committee of the Assembly. At the 1976 plenary session held at Williamsburg, Virginia, Representative Brooks was elected Vice President of the Assembly and was re-elected to that position at the 1977 and 1978 meetings. Other U.S. members elected to leading positions in the Assembly are Representative Burton, since 1978 as Chairman of the Political Committee and Representative Charles Rose, of North Carolina, since 1977 as Chairman of the Scientific and Technical Committee. At the 1978 meeting, Senator Sam Nunn of Kentucky was elected Vice-Chairman of the Military Committee and Senator Robert B. Morgan of North Carolina was elected Vice-Chairman of the Economic Committee.

The Canada-United States Interparliamentary Group was established by Congress under Public Law 86–42. Senator Edward Zorinsky of Nebraska and Representative Dante Fascell of Florida served as Cochairmen for the Twentieth Canada-United States Interparliamentary Conference in Canada in 1979.

The Mexico-United States Interparliamentary Group was established under Public Law 86–420. Senator Lloyd Bentsen of Texas and Representative E. (Kika) de la Garza of Texas served as Cochairmen for the nineteenth Mexico-United States Interparliamentary Conference in Mexico in 1979.

In addition to the above-mentioned interparliamentary groups which are specifically authorized and established by Congressional resolutions, a number of regular exchanges take place on a less formalized basis—under the general aegis of the House Committee on Foreign Affairs and its Chairman, Representative Clement J. Zablocki.

For the past seven years, for instance, a delegation of the House of Representatives has met on a biannual basis with a delegation of the European Parliament. The parliament is one of four institutions which collectively run the nine-nation European Community. (The other institutions are: the Commission, the Council of Ministers, and the Court of Justice.) This exchange takes on particular importance in the light of the "direct elections" which were held in June, 1979—whereby some 175 million European voters for the first time in history directly elected 410 representatives to an expanded European Parliament.

The Chairman of the United States delegation to the last (15th) meeting with the Europeans was Representative Donald J. Pease. Cochairmen were Representatives Sam Gibbons and Larry Winn, Jr.

Other interparliamentary groups in this (informal) category include: the British-American Interparliamentary Group (which meets alternately with House and Senate delegations on a biannual basis) and the France-United States Friendship Group which normally meets every other year.

As noted previously, the House Committee on Foreign Affairs and the Senate Committee on Foreign Relations regularly receive numerous *ad hoc* parliamentary delegations from many nations of the world—often as a followup to invitations extended to United States Members of Congress and Senators by foreign governments and legislatures. These exchanges, together with those of an institutionalized nature, are important elements in the interparliamentary consultative process.

From the Assembly of the Azores, President Alvaro Monjardino in conversation with Portuguese Ambassador João Hail Themido and Senator Claiborne Pell of Rhode Island.

Vice Premier Deng Xiao Ping, of the People's Republic of China, joins in the applause at a tea meeting in his honor. Also among those present are House Majority Leader James C. Wright of Texas and Speaker Thomas P. O'Neill of Massachusetts. January, 1979.

His Excellency Constantine Caramanlis, Prime Minister of Greece, prepares to address guests at a luncheon, during his State visit. Seated at the table are Majority Leader James C. Wright of Texas and chairman of the House Committee on Foreign affairs. Clement J. Zablocki of Wisconsin. June, 1978

A delegation from the Supreme Soviet of the U.S.S.R., headed by Boris N. Ponomarev, began a 10-day visit to the United States with this official luncheon. Speaker Thomas P. O'Neill of Massachusetts is seated at the left, and House Foreign Affairs Committee Chairman Clement J. Zablocki of Wisconsin stands at the right. January, 1978.

Prime Minister Menachem Begin of Israel in Washington to sign a peace treaty between the Arab Republic of Egypt and the State of Israel, March 1979. Standing with him are Minority Leader John J. Rhodes of Arizona, Speaker Thomas P. O'Neill of Massachusetts, House Foreign Affairs Committee Chairman Clement J. Zablocki of Wisconsin and House Majority Whip John Brademas of Indiana.

His Holiness John Paul II addresses Members of Congress on his October 1979 visit to the Nation's Capitol.

Norway's Prime Minister Odvar Nordli and Foreign Minister Knut Freydenlund share a toast to Norwegian-Americans with Senator George McGovern of South Dakota. June, 1979.

President Anwar Sadat of the Arab Republic of Egypt at a ceremonial reception which marked the signing of a peace treaty between his nation and the State of Israel, in March, 1979. With him are House Majority Leader James C. Wright of Texas, Speaker Thomas P. O'Neill of Massachusetts, House Minority Leader John J. Rhodes of Arizona and House Foreign Affairs Committee Chairman Clement J. Zablocki of Wisconsin.

His Excellency, Julius K. Nyerere, President of the United Republic of Tanzania, with the late Senator Humphrey of Minnesota, the late Representative Leo J. Ryan of California.

Her Majesty Elizabeth II, Queen of England with His Royal Highness Prince Philip, Duke of Edinburgh, Vice-President Nelson Rockefeller, Speaker Carl Albert and others, at a luncheon in Her Majesty's honor. As part of our Bicentennial celebration, England had sent with its Queen the Magna Carta for display in the United States, July, 1976.

Mayor Jacques Chirac of Paris, France, addressing the members of the North Atlantic Assembly. At left, Representative Jack Brooks of Texas, the Vice President of the Assembly.

Prime Minister of Japan Masayoshi Ohira is greeted by House Speaker Thomas P. O'Neill of Massachusetts and House Foreign Affairs Committee Chairman Clement J. Zablocki of Wisconsin. May, 1979.

The House Foreign Affairs Committee and Senate Foreign Relations Committee joined in holding a tea meeting to honor His Majesty King Hassan II of Morocco. Speaker Thomas P. O'Neill of Massachusetts and Senate Foreign Relations Committee Chairman Frank Church of Idaho stand with him. November, 1978.

153

The Modern Congress

Congress in the last decade has continued the traditions and procedures developed over the years; however, at the same time it has shown that Congress is a living institution. During this decade not only the membership has changed but also the traditions and procedures, where there was valid reason for change. New technology and management practices were adopted where feasible and Members of Congress began a major effort to keep themselves, and their staffs, better informed. Actions underway in the 96th Congress, as the decade ends, promise that these changes will serve as the foundation for additional improvements in the years ahead.

Background

Congress is a living, dynamic institution. Sometimes slowly, sometimes rapidly, Congressional membership, organization and procedures are constantly changing under the impact of the shifting economic, political and social circumstances of the nation. As one scholar has put it, Congress is in a perpetual state of reform. Even so, the pace of Congressional change was unusually rapid in the 1970s and thus the institution is different in many significant ways from what it was a decade ago.

Some fundamental Congressional features have changed very little. The basic constitutional structure and powers of Congress have not been much altered since the House of Representatives and the Senate first convened in 1789. Representatives are still elected to two-year terms and Senators to six-year terms, for example, although Senators are now directly chosen by the people instead of by State legislatures as they were before 1914. Both Houses still maintain a system of standing committees to study bills on particular subjects and recommend whether they should become law, and some of those

committees have existed continuously since the early 19th century. Most of the basic rules and procedures developed in the last century for debating and amending bills on the floors of the House and the Senate are still used today. The two Houses continue to apply the same means for reconciling their differences on legislation and for monitoring how the executive branch interprets and enforces acts of Congress.

On the other hand, long-term national population shifts have profoundly affected the composition of Congress and the work of its Members. The size of the House has increased from only 65 in the First Congress to the present total of 435, plus Delegates from the District of Columbia, Guam, and the Virgin Islands, and the Resident Commissioner from Puerto Rico. The Senate has also expanded as new States have entered the Union.

Moreover, the number of individuals each Member represents has grown enormously. Between 1800 and 1970 the average population in House districts shot up from about 34,000 to

Need a room for an official meeting? See pages 12 and 13.

The *Congressional Staff Journal* provides useful information to the staffs of the Congress embracing a broad range of professional activities and interests.

Booklets such as these help the congressional staff and the public gain an understanding of the offices of the Senate.

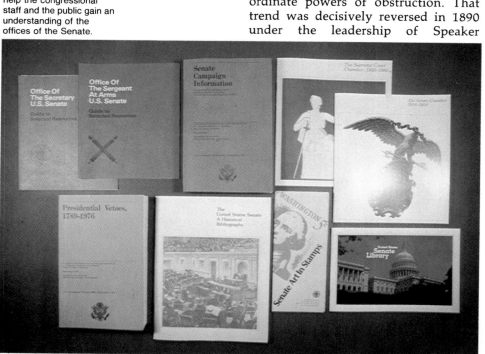

more then 467,000, and it will probably top the half-million mark by the 1980s. Also, as late as 1962 the actual populations of Congressional districts varied widely, in some instances by as much as 800,000 people. Supreme Court decisions of the mid-1960s corrected that inequity; today most district population sizes are as nearly equal as possible, given the constitutional requirement that every State must have at least one Representative no matter how small its population. The sharp increases in the number of people represented have been accompanied in recent decades by rising constituent demands for additional services from their Representatives and Senators, considerably expanding each legislator's workload. This growth has contributed to the pressure for expanded staff and physical space on Capitol Hill.

Furthermore, as more Americans have moved from rural to urban areas the number of city and suburban Congressional districts has increased while that of predominantly farming districts has declined. At the same time significant population shifts from frostbelt to sunbelt States have inexorably brought more House seats to the south, southwest and west at the expense of the northeast and midwest.

From time to time both Houses of Congress have significantly altered their rules and procedures. During the 19th century the minority in the House of Representatives acquired inordinate powers of obstruction. That trend was decisively reversed in 1890 under the leadership of Speaker Thomas B. Reed. From that time forward both parties have accepted the principle that, while protecting legitimate minority rights, the rules of the House must not prevent the majority from enacting its legislative proposals. Shortly after the turn of the century the House curtailed the powers of its Speaker, removing him from the chairmanship of the powerful Rules Committee and stripping him of the power to appoint all committee chairmen and members. A few years later the Senate adopted its first permanent cloture procedure to limit filibusters.

Other piecemeal changes continued to be made until 1946, when the Congress enacted a comprehensive Legislative Reorganization Act. Among its other achievements, this milestone of recent Congressional history sharply reduced the number of House and Senate committees, improved committee procedures, authorized professional staff for all committees, strengthened Congressional research agencies, modified the appropriations process, shifted responsibility for settling minor claims against the government to executive agencies and the courts, thereby considerably reducing the petty workload of Congress, and formally established oversight of the executive branch as a continuing statutory responsibility of the legislature. The Act also established a new Congressional procedure for dealing with the budget.

During the two decades that followed, Congress absorbed, modified, and considered the consequences of the 1946 Act. By reducing the number of committees and expanding the breadth of subjects under the jurisdiction of each, the Act had enhanced the influence of their chairmen. The stature of these powerful figures was further strengthened by invariable adherence to the seniority system which virtually guaranteed chairmanships to the committees' most senior majority party members. Following the consolidation of the committees, the number of subcommittees grew rapidly in both Houses. In the Senate, periodic battles erupted over proposals to strengthen cloture and the rule was twice modified. The House adopted rules to protect the rights of witnesses appearing before investigating committees and took steps to give the majority party's leadership greater influence over the Rules Committee. Meanwhile, Congress had abandoned the new budget process after two years' experience with it.

Into the 70s

The momentum for a new surge of Congressional change began to build in the mid-1960s. In 1965 both Houses agreed to the creation of a joint committee to restudy the whole structure and operation of the legislative branch and to make comprehensive recommendations. Many of these were incorporated into the Legislative Reorganization Act of 1970 which inaugurated a decade of numerous and far-reaching changes in almost every major feature of the legislature. Much of the impetus for this burst of transformations was supplied by the unusually large new generation of legislators that flooded into Congress in the 1970s. By 1979 two-thirds of the Representatives and about 61 percent of the Senators had served in their respective Houses only since 1970.

The power and influence of committee chairmen received particular attention during the 1970s. The 1970 Act gave committee Members a larger voice in committee proceedings. During the next several years, party caucuses eased the rigidity of the seniority system by making the appointment of chairman subject to biennial election. In the House, committee chairmen lost control over the organization, membership, jurisdictions, and staff of subcommittees. Furthermore, both Houses adopted rules that distributed chairmanships and committee seats more widely among their Members.

Committee jurisdiction was another subject of deep concern. Unforeseen in 1946, the emergence of such new national problems as energy, environ-mental protection and health care strained the ability of the committee system to produce coordinated and comprehensive policies. The 1970 Act made a few minor changes in the Senate's system; major alterations were agreed to in 1977. The House modified its system somewhat in 1974 and appointed a select committee to restudy the situation in 1979.

Both Houses took steps to speed up the legislative process in the 1970s. In the Senate it became the normal practice to consider almost every important bill under unanimous consent agreements that limited debate. To cope with situations in which such agreements could not be concluded, the Senate repeatedly strengthened its cloture rule: in 1975, 1976, and again in 1979. Meanwhile the House was amending its rules to restrict delaying tactics and to increase the use of procedures for expeditious consideration of legislation.

Major strides were taken during the 1970s to open the workings of Con-

A random sampling of reference publications prepared by caucuses and legislative support organizations in order to provide Members with information on various policy issues.

A staff person has numerous manuals and directories to assist them in the performance of their duties.

Training and education programs for staff, such as this Minority Legislative Education Program, are part of the everyday congressional life.

gress to the public view and to improve communication between Members and their constituents. Before this decade most committee meetings were held behind closed doors. Today, with few exceptions, committee meetings and hearings are conducted "in the sunshine," to promote better public understanding of national issues and proposals for responding to them. Committees may now permit radio and television coverage of their activities; the Senate has experimented with radio broadcasts of its floor debates; and the House has begun to televise its floor debates.

Votes that once went unrecorded are now a matter of public record, and the *Congressional Record* has been made a more accurate transcript of Congressional proceedings. New facilities and technologies have been developed to enable Representatives and Senators to explain their views and actions to their constituents, both from Washington and while at home. And Congress has adopted new codes of financial disclosure and standards of conduct to assure that legislators and their staffs are free from any taint of conflict of interest.

As the issues facing Congress grew in number and complexity, the legislature expanded its resources. Congressional staffs were enlarged to assist Members and committees in formulating policies and reviewing their implementation. Major new responsibilities were assigned to the General Accounting Office and to the Congressional Research Service of the Library of Congress. The Congressional Budget Office was established to provide expert information on national economic trends and their

implications for Congressional spending and taxing decisions. An Office of Technology Assessment was created to analyze the impact of technological developments on present and future public policies. These staffs and legislative agencies combine to provide Congress with comprehensive, expert and independent support facilities superior to those of any other legislature in the world.

Congress also took several major steps to reassert its great constitutional powers during the 1970s. In 1973, for example, the legislature adopted the War Powers Resolution, which clarified the respective roles of the President and the Congress in cases of threatened or undeclared hostilities. The Congressional Budget and Impoundment Control Act was passed in the following year to provide Congress with a better procedure for establishing spending priorities and improving the coordination of spending and taxing policies.

Furthermore, the 1970s engendered in Congress a heightened concern about its oversight capabilities and performance. It has always been understood that Congressional responsibilities extend beyond the making of laws, that monitoring the executive branch's execution of the laws is an equally significant duty. That task became even more crucial as the Federal Government grew to its present mammoth proportions, and Federal programs, activities and policies increasingly affected the lives of virtually every American. Congress responded to its new needs in the 1970s with new laws and rules encouraging its committees to do more, and more comprehensive, oversight. It also expanded the authority and resources of Congressional support agencies to assist committees in that task. By the end of the decade it was also considering several proposed new procedures to expand oversight activities even further.

Clearly Congress must and will continue to change. In no other way can it remain a vital and responsive instrument of democratic government. But the history of the institution reveals an underlying continuity, a devotion to the constitutional framework within which it was created. If the past is a reliable guide to the future, Congress will probably continue to confine its ceaseless evolution within the bounds of that stable and tested framework.

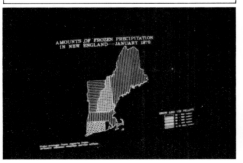

Through the use of computer graphics a Member can transform large amounts of statistical data into a graphic format that can be more readily understood.

Using Technology in Congress

A "fisheye" view of one of the data processing centers which help the modern Congress assimilate the large amount of information it receives daily.

The Congress has become an increasingly demanding environment where legislation, committee activities and constituent interests vie for Members' time and attention. At the same time, the issues confronting the Nation have grown more complex. These trends led Congress to look for new approaches to traditional tasks.

Modern computers, telecommunications, microforms and audio-video devices, as well as the associated new information management techniques, have proved to be valuable aids in support of administrative operations as well as for research and analysis. There is continuing interest in exploring new avenues for improving the efficiency of Congressional operations and enhancing the quality of information available to legislators. To meet this demand, the House, Senate and the Library of Congress now have professional staffs and sophisticated machine capabilities supporting the introduction and maintenance of needed technical services.

Budget and Policy Analysis

A broad spectrum of budget analysis and monitoring projects have been developed to support the House and Senate Committees on the Budget and Appropriations, the Congressional Budget Office and House and Senate authorizing committees since the passage of the Congressional Budget and Impoundment Control Act of 1974. Effective computer services are now available for committees and offices involved in budget formulation, analysis and tracking which show the impact that specific legislation can have on the total budget. These systems and an increasing number of computer-assisted models, are employed to help formulate policy alternatives, determine the long-range impact of proposed legislation, and enhance the oversight capabilities of Congress.

Computer graphics capability allows Members to have visual comparisons of budget figures, providing them with a better understanding of the overall Federal budget.

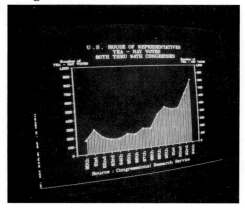

Automated Text-Editing and Electronic Printing

Through the use of automated text-editing systems, Congress can now eliminate many of the tedious clerical tasks associated with editing and revising long documents. In addition, both the House and Senate now utilize the electronic printing equipment of the Government Printing Office (GPO) for such things as bill processing, committee calendar preparation and hearings publication. At the same time, initiatives have been undertaken to improve the design of Congressional documents, to improve clarity of organization, increase readability and control costs.

Electronic Voting

Automated voting procedures were first employed in the House of Representatives in January 1973. The electronic voting system was installed in an effort to reduce the time required by the House voting process. The system shows information on votes in progress; running totals of Yea, Nay and Present responses; the time remaining during the voting period; and identification of the vote or quorum under consideration, on displays in the Chamber. It also assists in various clerical tasks associated with the voting process, including printing copies of the final vote results for distribution.

Legislative Information and Research Systems

The increase in legislative workload and the changing legislative process require a significant amount of record-keeping and research activities by Members and committees. In response to this need, several automated information resources have been made available. These systems include:

LEGIS—a system which tracks all House and Senate bills and resolutions
SCORPIO—information resources providing bibliographic information, analysis of major policy issues and abstracts of the *Congressional Record*
SOPAD—provides summaries of House Chamber proceedings within minutes
MBIS—provides current year and historical data on the Federal budget process
FAPRS—used for researching Federal assistance programs
JURIS—provides access to the U.S. Code.

By using a computer terminal in the office, a Congressional staff person can make an inquiry regarding the status of a piece of legislation and receive a response on the terminal's screen in a matter of seconds.

Modern tools and techniques are valuable aids to the offices of Congress in providing quick and efficient services.

By using a computer terminal in their Member's office, a House or Senate staff person can check computerized information resources maintained at the Library of Congress.

Located below the galleries on each side of the House Chamber, summary display panels present running tabulations as well as the time remaining for the vote in progress.

The House electronic voting system maintains voting stations, such as pictured here, in numerous locations throughout the House Chamber. By inserting their identification card, Representatives activate the voting system which allows them to cast their vote.

An individual Representative's vote is displayed on panels above the Speaker's chair while a vote is in progress in the House Chamber.

Senator Howard W. Cannon, of Nevada, searches a computerized information data base with the assistance of a Senate staff person. The professional staff of the House, Senate, and Library of Congress routinely provide orientation and training services to Members and their staff in the use of computer terminals and other modern office equipment.

Administrative Support Services

Although not highly visible, a variety of automated services support administrative functions of the Congress. These activities enable the Congress to function in a more orderly and cost-effective manner. Among the administrative functions receiving computer assistance are the keeping of personnel and payroll records, equipment inventory files and the performance of other financial management activities.

Member and Committee Office Automation

Computer systems now provide the means to assist Member and committee offices in establishing orderly, efficient and cost-effective operations. A substantial amount of time is often required for Members to respond to constituent queries on specific legislative issues and requests for assistance. Use of automated systems for correspondence management, text preparation, document revision, financial and inventory control, and scheduling of activities has been beneficial for establishing modern management procedures in Congressional offices.

Orientation and Training

The successful employment of new technologies depends on the proper orientation and adequate training of Members and staff in their use. The House, Senate, and the Congressional Research Service provide a series of cooperative comprehensive courses in retrieval of information from the variety of systems available throughout Congress. Information professionals conduct classroom session, including practice using computer terminal equipment, as well as distribute training manuals. Continuing education is also provided as new additions are made to Congressional data bases and assistance is available at all times to users with computer terminal difficulties or who have general questions about system performance or resources.

Micrographics

Micrographics technology has been used on Capitol Hill for many years for archival purposes. Currently, new day-to-day uses of various microforms are being explored in Member and committee offices, as well as in such administrative units as the Secretary of the Senate, the Clerk of the House and the Architect of the Capitol. Storage of materials in microforms offers the advantages of reducing storage space, providing duplicate copies at minimal cost and eliminating certain tedious filing tasks.

A Senate staff person uses a microfilm reader-printer to check archival files which have been put on microfilm in order to save space and time.

Audio-Video

The use of audio and video media for transferring information has become increasingly popular within the legislative setting. Greater public interest has been expressed in the activities of the Congress and this interest has been important in the movement toward televising floor proceedings and committee hearings. The House of Representatives now makes available television coverage of its floor proceedings, and the Senate makes available audio coverage of its floor proceedings to each Senator's office. Live coverage of Senate and House hearings on topics of special interest are also broadcast on certain occasions. In the Senate, audio coverage of the floor debate on the Panama Canal Treaty in 1978 was well received by the public and served as a pilot effort in this area.

Another use of audio-video techniques is in providing briefings to Members of Congress and their staffs. The Congressional Research Service offers several of its Issue Briefs in audio cassette form and has produced a limited number of video briefings on topics of critical interest to Congress. Also of note is the potential of-fered by videoconferencing via satellite. This technique was successfully demonstrated in the 95th Congress when the Senate Subcommittee on Science, Technology and Space was linked to witnesses commenting on artificial weather modification, situated in Springfield, Illinois. Another session provided the opportunity for a Member of Congress to talk to a group of students in his home district. As indicated by this experiment, Congress continues to explore the potential offered by new techniques and technologies for improving two-way communications between legislators and their constituents.

Television cameras provide coverage of House floor proceedings.

Through the use of television, Members of Congress such as Representative Charles Rose of North Carolina, are able to report periodically to their constituency.

Presidential Transition

The honor of your presence
is requested at the ceremonies
attending the Inauguration of the
President and Vice President
of the United States
January twentieth
Nineteen hundred seventy-seven

Howard W. Cannon, Chairman,
Robert C. Byrd, Mark O. Hatfield,
Thomas P. O'Neill, Jr., Jim Wright,
John J. Rhodes,
Committee on Arrangements.

Please present the enclosed
card of admission.   11:30 A.M.

Invitation for Inaugural
Ceremonies sent by the
Congressional Committee
on Arrangements.

The Inauguration of the
39th President of the
United States James Earl
Carter on the East Front of
the Capitol.
January 20, 1977.

The President-elect is escorted to the inaugural stand by Leaders of the Congress and elected officers of the House and Senate.

A very special guest arrives for the inaugural ceremonies—Amy Carter.

President Carter and former President Gerald R. Ford at the White House on Inauguration Day.

Mrs. Jimmy Carter and Mrs. Walter Mondale arrive for inaugural ceremonies.

167

Chief Justice of the United States Warren E. Burger administers the Presidential oath of office to James Earl Carter while Mrs. Carter holds the Bible on January 20, 1977.

President Jimmy Carter delivers his inaugural speech as former President Ford and former Vice President Rockefeller listen.

Former President Ford congratulates President Carter as the lights from the press glare.

Former President & Mrs. Ford leave the West Front of the Capitol by helicopter after the inaugural ceremonies.

President and Mrs. Carter walk the inaugural route to the White House from the Capitol.

Vice President-elect Walter F. Mondale (center), is escorted on inauguration day by Kenneth R. Harding (lower left), Sergeant at Arms of the House of Representatives; F. Nordy Hoffmann (lower right), Sergeant at Arms of the Senate; Representative James C. Wright of Texas, (upper left) House Majority Leader; and Senator Robert C. Byrd of West Virginia (upper right), Senate Majority Leader.

Working Relationships

President Jimmy Carter addresses the Congress.

Speaker Thomas P. O'Neill, Jr., of Massachusetts introduces the President of the United States, Jimmy Carter, to a joint session of Congress.

The relationship between the Congress and the President is intricate and complex. In theory, their powers and responsibilities are separated; in fact, their roles overlap. Thus, although the Constitution vests all legislative authority in the Congress, the President has important powers and responsibilities—both constitutional and customary—in the formulation and enactment of legislation. And while the Constitution gives the executive authority to the President, it also empowers Congress to check the President's actions in many ways.

Under the Constitution, the President must inform the Congress periodically on the state of the Union; he usually does so annually. The President may also transmit to Congress special messages and reports on particular subjects, and he often sends to "the Hill" actual drafts of bills. He may exercise his veto power, threaten to do so, or appeal personally and directly to Congressional leaders and individual Members of Congress to persuade them to support his programs. His authority to adjourn Congressional sessions in case of disagreement between the two Houses has never been exercised, but he has occasionally used his power to call either or both Houses into "special" session, although rarely since the 1920s. The last such session was called in 1948 during the Truman Administration.

The President's state of the Union message to Congress receives wide public attention. Although the time, place, and manner of transmitting it is discretionary with each President, he customarily delivers the message in person at the opening of each session of Congress. Quite often it contains his views on significant matters requiring legislative attention and on the kind of legislation he wants Congress to enact. With the advent of television, this annual speech has been increasingly addressed to the people of America and of the world as well as to the Congress. It is a solemn occasion of state; modern Presidents have used it to dramatize their aims and policies and to gain Congressional support for their recommendations.

Soon after delivering the state of the Union address, the President sends to Congress his annual budget message and economic report. These are normally delivered in writing rather

The Vice President and President of the Senate Walter F. Mondale and Speaker of the House, Thomas P. O'Neill, Jr., applaud President Carter.

The last three Presidents to work with the Congress (left to right) President Jimmy Carter and former Presidents Gerald R. Ford and Richard M. Nixon.

than in person. All Presidents send numerous other special messages to the Congress at various times during a Congressional session. Ordinarily these cover some special subject and are designed and timed to enhance support for the President's legislative agenda. Occasionally, the President delivers a special message in person to emphasize the subject's vital importance. He may be warning a foreign nation of possible American reaction to its behavior, or he may be interpreting or summarizing American views for the benefit of the rest of the world.

In addition to these various messages, the President and executive agencies often send draft legislation to the Congress. Members of Congress usually introduce these items at the request of the President because neither he nor any executive official may do so.

How much effect these and other Presidential actions have in persuading Congress to accept his recommendations depends upon the circumstances. Congress is under no legal obligation to follow the President's lead, and

often does not. It may or may not act; if it acts, it may do so in accord with or directly opposite to the President's stated wishes. Few major Presidential proposals survive the legislative process unchanged. Every President eventually learns that while the President proposes, the Congress disposes.

Constitutionally, the President has four courses of action when Congress submits a bill or joint resolution for his signature. He may sign it into law. He may hold it for up to ten days, whereupon, if Congress is still in session, it becomes law without his signature. If Congress adjourns during the ten-day period, the measure dies if the President has failed to sign it. This "pocket veto" is absolute and cannot be overridden by the Congress. Finally, the President may veto a measure by returning it to Congress without his signature and with a statement of the reasons for his disapproval. Congress may override the President's veto by a two-thirds vote in each House, whereupon the measure becomes law without the President's signature. If Congress does not override the veto, it will often redraft the legislation and try to work with the Administration until an agreement can be reached.

The President often meets informally with the leaders and other Members of Congress not only to discuss legislation, but also to exchange ideas and opinions on current events, problems and matters of importance to the Nation. Frequently, the President invites Members to the White House for briefings and sends his aides to Capitol Hill for the same purpose. The Congressional leadership is usually invited to the White House to be informed of major Presidential decisions and actions or important events before they are announced to the rest of the country and the world.

The relationship between the executive and legislative branches of our Government is sometimes marked with conflict, often characterized by compromise, and sometimes strained. Nevertheless, the two branches usually strive to work harmoniously for the best interests of the Nation and the welfare of its people.

The President welcomes Speaker Thomas P. O'Neill, Jr., of Massachusetts (left) and Senate Majority Leader Robert C. Byrd of West Virginia to the White House for a legislative briefing.

President enters the House Chamber to address the Congress with House Majority Leader Jim Wright of Texas, House Majority Whip, John Brademas, of Indiana, and House Minority Leader John Rhodes of Arizona. Chief Justice Warren E. Burger is behind the President.

President Carter meets with bipartisan Congressional leaders. (From left to right) Senator John Tower of Texas, Chairman, Republican Policy Committee; Representative James C. Wright of Texas, Majority Leader of the House; Senator Ted Stevens of Alaska, Minority Whip of the Senate; Speaker Thomas P. O'Neill of Massachusetts; President Carter; Senator Robert C. Byrd of West Virginia, Majority Leader of the Senate and Representative John J. Rhodes of Arizona, Minority Leader of the House.

A bill becomes a law. The President signs a bill into law as Members of Congress and the Cabinet witness the signing.

The White House. President Jimmy Carter discusses pending legislation; (left to right) Senator Jennings Randolph of West Virginia; Senate Majority Leader Robert Byrd of West Virginia; the President; Speaker Thomas P. O'Neill, Jr., of Massachusetts; House Majority Leader Jim Wright of Texas (back to camera) and Representative Frank Thompson, Jr., of New Jersey. (back to camera)

Legislative Support Agencies

Library of Congress

The Library of Congress is believed to be the largest repository of organized knowledge in the world. It was founded in 1800 to "furnish such books as may be necessary for the use of Congress". In the gray granite structure shown on these pages, and in an adjoining modern annex of Georgia white marble are housed more than 18

Daniel J. Boorstin, the Librarian of Congress.

The Great Hall in the Library of Congress

million books and pamphlets, together with more than 55 million manuscripts, maps, prints, photographs and other examples of man's graphic expression through the ages.

The Library's relationship to the Congress of the United States is unique. It is an immediately accessible and indispensable tool of the Members of Congress and their committees. Its first and foremost function is to serve them. The Library furnishes facts and reports on any subject they need. Any Member or committee may borrow the book or document needed, or may have it excerpted, pinpointed or analyzed by experts on the Library staff. One department alone, the Congressional Research Service, handled more than 300,000 congressional inquiries by phone during fiscal 1978. On a busy day, it is not unusual for more than 2,000 inquiries to be received. Many other congressional requests are answered by the Law Library, research services, divisions and other departments.

The Library was housed in the Capitol until 1897. It suffered two disastrous fires early in its history. The entire collection of some 3,000 books was destroyed during the War of 1812, when British troops temporarily occupied Washington and burned the Capitol on August 24, 1814. Congress promptly reconstituted the collections by purchasing the private library of Thomas Jefferson, some 6,000 volumes, on January 30, 1815. Jefferson had spent nearly 50 years assembling these books, which he had carefully organized with his own system of classification. From this new beginning, the Library grew rapidly until December 24, 1851, when another fire destroyed about 35,000 volumes.

Since that time, the Library's growth has been uninterrupted. The purchase in 1867 of the Peter Force

collection of more than 60,000 books, pamphlets and other items of Americana was one of a number of notable acquisitions with which Congress enriched the collections of its Library. In 1930, Congress voted $1,500,000 for the purchase of the Vollbehr Collection of 3,000 fifteenth-century books, including the famous Gutenberg Bible, the first book printed on movable metal type. The transfer of the library of the Smithsonian Institution to the Library of Congress in 1866, and subsequent receipts through this source, have added more than a million volumes. In 1870 Congress assigned to the Library all duties connected with copyright, insuring that it would receive a large part of the literary and artistic production of the United States. Substantial gifts from private individuals also have increased enormously the Library's resources in books and manuscripts. Finally, a network of international exchange and purchases from overseas offices have brought in material from all over the world.

This continued expansion of the collections has dictated the expansion of the Library's physical plant as well. In the summer of 1980, the Library will more than double its available

One of the Library's many treasures: the contents of Lincoln's pockets the night he died.

During the War of 1812, the British burned the Library, which then was located in the Capitol.

The Library of Congress Building, with the Thomas Jefferson Building at the rear.

The Main Reading Room.

Outdoor concerts are just some of the many free cultural events at the Library.

space with the opening of the James Madison Memorial Building, immediately south of the main building on Independence Ave., S.E. The new building is the size of a full city block. It will contain numerous reading rooms, exhibit halls, and facilities for book storage, in addition to a memorial hall honoring James Madison, the chief author of the Bill of Rights and fourth President of the United States.

The Library's total contents in 1978 amounted to well over 73 million items. In addition to more than 18 million printed volumes and pamphlets, there are more than 74,000 bound newspaper volumes, 252,000 motion picture reels, 912,000 reels and strips of microfilm, and more than 32 million manuscripts relating to American history and civilization. Among the Library's greatest possessions are some of the most revered documents of American history, such as Jefferson's "rough draft" of the Declaration of Independence, one of the original copies of the Bill of Rights, and the first two drafts of the Gettysburg Address in Lincoln's handwriting. From these collections can be drawn the facts that are needed to frame informed legislation. The remainder are maps and views, music, fine prints and photographs, posters and broadsides.

The Library administers the national program of library services for the blind and physically handicapped, providing in 1978 free loan of braille and talking books and magazines to more than half a million blind and physically handicapped persons through a nationwide network of more than 160 cooperating libraries.

This institution also may be considered a business, for it earned $6,998,651 from the sale of catalog cards and kindred technical bibliographic materials to other libraries in fiscal year 1978. Another $3,495,681 came to it for copyright registration fees the same year. In addition, the Library is a cultural center, where concerts and lectures are presented. It also houses the school for Capitol pages.

The Library of Congress is an aggregate of many libraries. Its Law Library, for instance, is among the best in the United States. Much of its usefulness stems from the fact that new legislation grows from records of the past. This was recognized early in the Library's history when, in 1832, Congress established the law collection. Other notable collections include those of Japanese, Chinese, and Russian materials, the largest outside the Orient and the Soviet Union, respectively.

Daniel J. Boorstin, a distinguished American historian, educator and prize-winning author, presides over this unique combination of facilities and services as the Librarian of Congress. Nominated by President Ford and confirmed by the Senate on September 26, 1975, Dr. Boorstin is the 12th Librarian of Congress in the institution's history.

The Library's first priority is service to the Congress. But its doors are open to all people. Anyone can use the Library's collections, providing he is over high school age. Its exhibition halls are thronged with school children and other visitors. Its reading rooms attract scholars and students from all over the world. Its bibliographic, loan, and catalog distribution services are used by the entire library world.

The Congressional Research Service

The Congressional Research Service, a separate department within the Library, serves as one of the research arms of the Congress. The Service was first established in 1914 for the periods during which Congress was in session. As the complexities and the burden of the problems before Congress increased, its staff and functions were enlarged accordingly, comprising today a staff of more than 800 persons, including selected experts in such fields as law, economics, political science, international relations, natural sciences, and history. Senior specialists on the staff are frequently called upon to serve as consultants to Congressional committees. The Director of the Service, Gilbert Gude, is a former Maryland Congressman whose ten years of Congressional service place him in a unique position to anticipate and serve the needs of Congress.

Formerly called the Legislative Reference Service, the Congressional Research Service received its new name and greatly expanded responsibilities under legislation passed by Congress in 1970. The Service, at the beginning of each Congress, prepares and presents to each Congressional committee a list of subjects and policy areas related to its concerns and also a list of programs and activities scheduled to expire during that Congress. Upon request, the Service prepares legislative histories on measures to be considered in hearings; supplies committees with experts to prepare objective, nonpartisan analyses of legislative proposals that include evaluations of whether enactment of these or alternative proposals is advisable and the probable results of each; and gathers, analyzes and makes available to Members and committees other information needed in the performance of their duties. Also prepared regularly is a comprehensive digest of bills and resolutions of a public general nature introduced in either House.

Some of the various publications of the Congressional Research Service.

Gilbert Gude, Director, Congressional Research Service.

The staff of the Congressional Research Service prepare reports for Members of Congress.

The Juilliard String Quartet performs frequently in the Coolidge Auditorium of the Library.

Congressional Budget Office

In a major effort to reassert its constitutional authority over the Federal budget, the Congress in 1974 enacted a comprehensive budget reform measure, the Congressional Budget and Impoundment Control Act of 1974 (Public Law 93–344). The Budget Act set up a process whereby each year the Congress determines the appropriate level of Federal revenues, spending, and debt, and the size of the deficit through the passage of two concurrent resolutions on the budget.

Each spring, the Congress formulates and adopts a concurrent resolution setting budget targets for the fiscal year to begin on the coming October 1st. In September, the Congress reviews the detailed spending and revenue decisions it has made since the first resolution in the form of individual bills. It then arrives at and adopts a second concurrent resolution, reconfirming or changing the totals in the spring resolution. While the first resolution sets targets, the second establishes an actual ceiling on spending and a floor for revenues. If subsequent adjustments are required by changing circumstances, the Congress can enact additional concurrent resolutions.

The Budget Act created three new entities: Budget Committees in both the House and the Senate and the Congressional Budget Office (CBO). CBO is a nonpartisan organization mandated to provide the Congress with budget-related information and with analyses of alternative fiscal, budgetary and programmatic policies. The office does not make recommendations on matters of policy; its principal tasks are to present the Congress with options for consideration and to study the possible budgetary ramifications of those options.

The organization is headed by a Director who is appointed to a four-year term by the Speaker of the House and the President Pro Tempore of the Senate, after considering the recommendations of the Budget Committees. Dr. Alice Rivlin was named the first Director of CBO in February 1975. For fiscal year 1979, CBO was authorized a budget of $11,368,000 and a staff of 218 persons.

CBO's specific responsibilities include: estimates of the five-year budgetary costs of proposed legislation, inflation impact analyses of proposed legislation, tracking of Congressional budgetary actions against preset budget targets (scorekeeping), periodic forecasts of economic trends and alternative fiscal policies, studies of programmatic or policy issues that affect the Federal budget, and an annual report on major budgetary options.

Cost Estimates. The Budget Act requires the office to provide four types of cost estimates.

CBO prepares, to the extent practicable, a five-year estimate of what it would cost the Federal Government to carry out any public bill or resolution reported by Congressional committees (except the two appropriating committees).

Alice M. Rivlin, Director, Congressional Budget Office.

CBO furnishes to a reporting committee a report on each committee bill providing new budget authority. The report shows a comparison of the bill with the most recent concurrent resolution, a five-year projection of outlays associated with the bill, and the amount of new budget authority and resulting outlays provided for State and local governments.

The organization also furnishes to a reporting committee an analysis of each bill providing new or increased tax expenditures. The reports include an assessment of how the bill would affect levels of tax expenditures most recently detailed in a concurrent resolution, and a five-year projection of the tax expenditures resulting from the bill. As soon as practicable after the beginning of each fiscal year, CBO prepares a report that analyzes the five-year costs of continuing current Federal spending and taxing policies as set forth in the second concurrent resolution. The purpose of these projections is to provide a neutral baseline against which the Congress can consider potential changes as it examines the budget for the upcoming fiscal years.

Inflation Analysis. CBO prepares estimates of the inflationary effect of major legislative proposals; more generally, the office is charged with identifying then analyzing the causes of inflation. The estimates are intended to provide the Congress with guidelines about the cost in terms of inflation that new programs might entail.

Scorekeeping. The Office keeps track, or score, of Congressional action on individual bills, comparing the results of such action with the targets or ceilings in the concurrent resolutions. The office issues periodic reports showing the status of Congressional action.

Fiscal Analysis. Since the Federal budget both affects and is affected by the national economy, the Congress must consider the budget in the context of the current and projected state of the economy. To provide a framework for such considerations, CBO prepares periodic analyses and forecasts of economic trends. It also prepares analyses of alternative fiscal policies.

Program and Policy Analysis. CBO undertakes analyses of programmatic or policy issues that affect the Federal budget. These reports include an examination of alternative approaches to current policy; all reports are nonpartisan in nature. Major studies have been completed in such diverse areas as agriculture, energy, housing, hospital and medical costs, defense, State and local government, employment programs, transportation, education, and budget procedures.

Annual Report on Budget Options. By April 1 of each year, CBO furnishes to the House and Senate Committees on the Budget a report that combines many aspects of the functions outlined above. The annual report presents a discussion of alternative spending and revenue levels, levels of tax expenditures under existing law, and alternative allocations among major programs and functional categories.

CBO prepares its studies and cost estimates at the request of the Chairman or ranking minority member of a full committee of jurisdiction or the Chairman of a subcommittee of jurisdiction. The Budget Act establishes the following priority for these services: first, the Senate and House Budget Committees; second, the Senate and House Appropriations Committees, the Senate Finance Committee, and the House Ways and Means Committee; finally, all other Congressional committees.

The agency's published reports are distributed to all Members of Congress. Additional information and assistance are available through CBO's Office of Intergovernmental Relations.

CBO staff review a committee transcript regarding Federal appropriations.

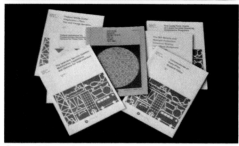

Some of the various publications of the Congressional Budget Office.

CBO staff are located in a Congressional Office Building along with other House committee offices.

CBO staff review computer reports on budget details.

Comptroller General Elmer B. Staats confers with Deputy Comptroller General Robert F. Keller before a hearing.

Comptroller General Elmer B. Staats is greeted by Senators Jim Sasser of Tennessee and Richard Schweiker of Pennsylvania, Chairman and Ranking Minority Member of the Senate Legislative Appropriations Subcommittee prior to a hearing.

GAO's Headquarters Building is the base from which its staff conducts reviews of Federal programs worldwide. Its location is convenient both to Capitol Hill and Cabinet department offices.

Finding ways to run the Federal Government—a $500 billion enterprise—more efficiently, effectively and economically is the task of the U.S. General Accounting Office.

The General Accounting Office came into existence as an independent, nonpolitical arm of the Congress in 1921 when the Budget and Accounting Act was enacted.

GAO's basic purposes are:

—To assist the Congress, its committees and its Members as much as possible in carrying out their legislative and oversight responsibilities, consistent with the agency's role as an independent, nonpolitical agency.

—To audit and evaluate the programs, activities and financial operations of Federal departments and agencies and make recommendations toward more efficient and effective operations.

—To carry out financial control and other functions with respect to Federal Government programs and operations including accounting, legal and claims settlement work.

GAO's primary internal objective is to perform all of its functions as effectively, efficiently, economically and promptly as possible.

Government has become much more complex since the Congress established GAO almost 60 years ago. The needs of the Congress for help have grown and will continue to grow.

This agency's greatest contribution is to provide answers to questions such as:

—Where are there opportunities to eliminate waste and the inefficient use of public money?

—Are Federal programs, whether administered directly by the Federal Government or through other organizations, such as the United Nations, or through State and local governments, achieving their objectives?

—Are there other ways of accomplishing the objectives of these programs at lower costs?

—Are funds being spent legally and is the accounting for them adequate?

Using such information, Members of Congress are in a better position to make decisions concerning Government programs—whether the issue is continuing an innovative education program, acquiring a major weapons system for the Defense Department or providing development assistance for a foreign country.

Concerns are being voiced in the Congress and elsewhere about the apparent decrease of confidence in the Government, particularly in the Government's ability to make programs effective and to serve well those individuals and groups for whom public funds are spent. Greater attention is also being focused on the accountability of Government officials to taxpayers. Thus it is more important than ever that the public be aware of the work of GAO as an organization with principal concern for fiscal integrity and the economical and effective management of Government programs.

Another concern frequently expressed in the Congress is that the executive branch has increased its power in relationship to the legislative branch for the simple reason that the executive branch has most of the experts and information on such complex subjects as major weapons systems, energy, space exploration, health care, and pollution control.

Many of these experts and much of the information from the executive branch are made available to the Congress through hearings and reports, or by less formal means. However, inevitable questions remain.

—Were the proper alternatives to proposed programs fully considered and

set forth objectively to the Congress?
—Does the executive branch keep the Congress adequately advised on progress and on problems which develop as programs are carried out?
—Does the information provided facilitate, rather than frustrate, legislative oversight?

Accordingly, one of GAO's objectives is to strengthen the processes through which the Congress can obtain reliable information.

In a broad context, the agency is responsible to the public. GAO reports to the Congress, if not classified for national security reasons, are public reports. Although GAO has no official ombudsman responsibility, it tries at all times to be sensitive to responsible criticisms of Federal programs and to take these criticisms into account in planning its work.

GAO does not seek publicity for its reports. But it is important that the public have full access to its findings and conclusions. GAO can provide the public with a demonstration of the openness of the governmental processes.

The agency recognizes that certain information must be classified in the interest of national security. The legal authority to classify information rests with the operating agencies. GAO has as one of its objectives, however, the questioning of security classifications which seem unnecessary for the purposes of security legislation and regulations.

The organization's role will continue to change as the needs of the Congress respond to the increasing size and complexity of our Nation and its Government.

GAO performs much of its work with the objective of improving Government operations. As a result of its recommendations, Federal agencies take many actions to make their programs and services more economical and effective.

It is not possible to determine the full effect of GAO activities in terms of financial savings, improvements in Government operations, and increased effectiveness of Government programs and activities. However, GAO attempts to record actions attributable to its work which result in dollar savings or other benefits to the Federal Government, contractors, grantees, and the general public. These actions may be taken directly by the agency, as in the case of claims collections. Usually, however, they are taken by the Congress, Federal agencies, and others, in response to suggestions and recommendations.

For fiscal year 1978, GAO identified estimated savings of $2.5 billion attributable to its work. At the same time, it should be remembered that many accomplishments cannot always be stated in precise dollar terms. Savings resulting from management improvements often cannot be measured accurately, nor can improvements which make programs work better but not cheaper. Such improvements are often more important than simple financial savings.

Early in its history, most GAO employees were accountants or auditors who spent long hours pouring over vouchers and other financial records of Government agencies. However, in the 1950s, the organization extended the scope of its reviews to include:
—checking for compliance with applicable laws and regulations,
—examining the efficiency and economy of operations, and
—reviewing the results of operations of evaluating whether desired results, including legislatively prescribed objectives, have been effectively achieved.

In the past years, GAO's professional staff—numbering 4,200—has been expanded to include engineers, mathematicians, statisticians, computer specialists, economists, business and public administrators, and even a medical doctor.

During fiscal year 1978, the agency issued 1,136 audit reports and special studies, addressed to the Congress, its committees or Members, or to heads of departments and agencies. Copies of these reports are available to the public through GAO's Distribution Section, Room 1518, 441 G Street, NW, Washington, D.C. 20548.

GAO provides information to the Congress by testifying before Congressional committees; holding informal briefings on agency problems for committees, Members and staffs; assigning staff members to work on Congressional committees; and providing legal opinions and comments on pending legislation.

In addition, the Office undertakes reviews of major Government programs on its own initiative. Although GAO is authorized to investigate all matters relating to the receipt, disbursement, and application of public funds (with some exceptions), the policy is to review programs, activities, or functions of direct interest to the Congress and the public.

Other GAO Responsibilities

GAO prescribes principles and standards for accounting in executive branch agencies, and cooperates with the agencies in developing and improving their accounting and financial management systems.

The office settles legal questions concerning the legality of planned expenditures of Federal funds.

Questions over the award of Government contracts may prompt requests for a Comptroller General ruling on the bid protest. GAO decisions on questions about the award of Government contracts are binding on the executive branch, but may be overturned by the Congress or the courts.

The agency also settles claims for or against the Government. Claims which involve no doubtful questions of law are paid or collected by the agency involved, subject to GAO audit.

Some Further Facts About GAO

The Comptroller General of the United States is the head of GAO. The Comptroller General is appointed by the President, with the advice and consent of the Senate, to a 15-year term—the longest set term in the Federal Government. He cannot be removed except for cause. These provisions guarantee his independence from political influence.

Elmer B. Staats has been Comptroller General since 1966.

He heads an operation that includes the headquarters office and about 60 audit sites in the Washington, D.C., area, 15 regional offices in the continental United States and branch offices in Bangkok, Frankfurt, Honolulu, and Panama City.

GAO publications are important informative and analytical documents for Congressional oversight.

Government Printing Office

The Government Printing Office, which produces the *Congressional Record* among its many printing requirements, is almost within the shadow of the Capitol.

Virtually in the shadow of the Capitol stands the United States Government Printing Office. This four-building complex at North Capitol and H Streets houses an impressive array of production equipment as well as warehousing for paper, laboratories for testing graphic arts materials, facilities for rail and motor shipping, and administrative offices. In all, 34 acres of floor space are used in this location. Another 8-plus acres of publications distribution and paper warehousing are rented in various locations. The Government Printing Office also operates five Regional Field Printing plants and 14 Regional Printing Procurement Offices throughout the United States.

The Government Printing Office began operation in 1861 to produce all printing, binding, and blank book work for Congress, the Executive Office, the Judiciary, other than the Supreme Court of the United States, and every executive department, independent office and establishment of the Federal Government. Buildings, equipment and machinery were acquired from Cornelius Wendell, a private printer, for $135,000. The original plant stood on the site now occupied by the newest of GPO's buildings and was staffed by a work force of 350. Today GPO employs more than 7,500 employees and has an annual payroll over $130 million.

The Record Press at the Government Printing Office busily turns out the *Congressional Record* as well as the *Federal Register* overnight.

Annual visit by Office of Management and Budget officials to GPO finds Public Printer John J. Boyle explaining production of The Budget of the United States to OMB Director James T. McIntyre, Jr., in press area.

More and more Government printing is being produced electronically, and at the Government Printing Office there is perhaps the most comprehensive electronic photocomposition equipment under one roof anywhere.

In fiscal year 1978 the GPO's volume of business exceeded $500 million. Of this amount, nearly $320 million of printing was procured from commercial firms which compete on the basis of price and service for Government work.

To meet the printing and binding needs of its more than 110 customers, all of which are agencies of the Federal Government, the Office operates 111 presses of various kinds, utilizes nearly 305 composing and casting machines, operates two Linotron photocomposers, three Video Comp 500, one Compugraphic 7500, and over 135 other photocomposing keyboards and converting devices. A total of 238 binding machines such as cutters, stitchers, gatherers, and sewing machines are used to manufacture finished documents and hard-bound books.

The GPO operates around the clock, the needs of Congress comprising the most important of its nighttime production. Foremost among those needs is printing the indispensable Proceedings and Debates of the Congress, better known as the *Congressional Record.* This publication, printed each day when either of the Houses is in session, currently averages more than 300 pages daily. It consists of four main parts: a chronicle of floor action in the Senate, the same for the House, an Extension of Remarks, and a Daily Digest. The Extension portion carries official and unofficial material pertinent to, but not properly a part of, chamber proceedings. The Daily Digest lists the highlights of current legislative business, committee meetings and the legislative program ahead. About 36,000 copies of the *Record* are produced daily from newly set type.

Copy begins flowing to the GPO around 6:00 p.m. each day and concurrently the GPO production staff begins building up to accommodate the influx. By midnight, all copy is supposed to be in the Office but at times this deadline is exceeded by late-arriving material. It is not uncommon for every one of GPO's composing machines to be manned in order to get all copy set into type in sufficient time to allow for lockup, plating, press-running time, and finishing operations. All operations are keyed to meeting fixed early morning delivery schedules which insure that Members of Congress and their staffs receive copies of the *Record* promptly.

But not only does the Government Printing Office carry out its printing and publications functions, it also operates a sizable distribution and sales program.

The Documents area, established in 1895 as an organic part of the GPO, performs this function. In Fiscal 1978, this department distributed more than 148 million publications, including nearly 14.5 million to Depository Libraries, and sold nearly 46 million documents to the public, chiefly through its mail order service. Twenty-five bookstores, 19 of which are located outside the metropolitan Washington area, sold more than $6 million worth of publications. On an appropriation of $23 million (the rest of the GPO operates on a revolving fund), the Public Documents Department's income was nearly $44 million from mail order and bookstore sales.

The GPO, properly called the largest general printing plant in the world under one roof, averages in excess of 1,800 new orders daily. Federal printing is directly responsive to the needs of the Government and as America grows and prospers, its progress will continue to be mirrored in its printing.

In addition to some 1,800 mail requests for publications as well as for information, the Government Printing Office handles countless telephone calls in its Documents Information Center.

Liaison between the Government Printing Office and the Congress is accomplished by the Congressional Information Office at the GPO.

Representative Frank Thompson, Jr., left, of New Jersey and Senator Claiborne Pell of Rhode Island serve as the Chairman and the Vice Chairman of the Joint Committee on Printing which is GPO's governing body.

Typography and Design division planning design for this issue of *The Capitol.*

Distributing documents is a mammoth task at the Government Printing Office. One of the busiest operations is at the Eisenhower warehouse in Alexandria, the site of GPO's Library and Statutory Distribution Service.

Office of Technology Assessment

Chairman, Representative
Morris K. Udall of Arizona

Vice Chairman, Senator
Ted Stevens of Alaska

Dr. John Gibbons,
Director of OTA

The Office of Technology Assessment (OTA) was established in 1972 as an advisory arm to the U.S. Congress (Public Law 92–484). OTA's basic function is to help legislators anticipate and plan for the long-term consequences of technological applications, and to examine the many ways, expected and unexpected, in which technology affects people's lives.

The agency's analyses explore the physical, biological, economic, social and political impacts which can result from application of scientific knowledge. OTA provides Congress with independent and timely information about the potential effects and side effects—both beneficial and harmful—of technological applications.

The OTA Act provides that assessments may be initiated by committee request, by the OTA Congressional Board or by the Director in consultation with the Board. The Office presents objective and detailed policy analyses and options to Congress, leaving decisions to the elected Members. OTA reports are also made available to the public through the U.S. Government Printing Office and the National Technical Information Service.

OTA consists of a bipartisan Congressional Board "which shall formulate and promulgate the policies of the Office and a Director who shall carry out such policies and administer the operations of the Office". The Board is assisted by an Advisory Council composed of 10 citizens from the private sector and, ex officio, the Comptroller General of the United States and the Director of the Congressional Research Service of the Library of Congress.

The Congressional Board consists of six Senators and six Representatives, evenly divided by party, and the Direc-

Publications of the Office
of Technology
Assessment.

tor, who serves on the Board, ex officio. Congressman Morris K. Udall (D-Arizona) is the Chairman and Senator Ted Stevens (R-Alaska) is the Vice Chairman during the 96th Congress. The chairmanship and vice-chairmanship alternate between the two Houses with each Congress.

The Director of OTA is Dr. John H. Gibbons. Prior to becoming OTA Director, he was Director of the University of Tennessee Environmental Center. Earlier, he headed the Environmental Program at Oak Ridge National Laboratory, and had been Director of the Office of Energy Conservation, Federal Energy Administration.

The Chairman of the Advisory Council is Frederick C. Robbins, Dean, Case Western Reserve Medical School and Nobel Laureate. The Vice Chairman is Jerome B. Wiesner, President of the Massachusetts Institute of Technology and former Science Advisor to the President.

The Office comprises three assessment divisions with an Assistant Director heading each division. The divisions are: Energy, Materials, and Global Security; Health and Life Sciences; and Science, Information, and Transportation. Reflecting Congressional concerns, OTA conducts, within these divisions, projects in the fields of energy, food, genetics and population, health, materials, national security, R&D policies and priorities, oceans, space technology, technology and international relations, telecommunications and information systems, and transportation.

Operating with a budget of $11 million for fiscal year 1979, the Office typically has underway some 30 projects at any given time. OTA complements its staff with the aid of technical or business experts and public-interest spokespersons, who reflect a wide variety of labor, management, consumer, governmental, environmental and geographic points of view. Last year, the agency completed studies on a number of issues, including: solar energy, medical technologies, coal slurry pipelines, and nutrition.

Public participation meeting at OTA

Members of the Joint Office of Technology Assessment Advisory Committee (TACC) and Congressional Board, left to right, Daniel De Simone, Deputy Director of OTA; Edward Wenk, Jr., TAAC member; Ronald Davenport, TAAC member; J. M. Leathers, TAAC member; Elmer Staats, TAAC member; Hazel Henderson, TAAC member; J. Fred Bucy, TAAC member; Russell Peterson, former director of OTA; Congressman George Brown, Jr., Member of OTA Congressional Board; Senator Edward M. Kennedy, Member of OTA Congressional Board; Jerome Wiesner, TAAC member; James Fletcher, TAAC member; Charles Kimball, TAAC member; John McAlister, Jr., TAAC member;

In Highest Tribute

There is no more appropriate place than the Rotunda of the Capitol to give honor to great servants of the people.

Flag at half mast over Capitol in highest tribute.

Four times in our history, assassination has claimed the occupant of the White House. A forced but orderly transition took place after the tragic deaths of Abraham Lincoln, James A. Garfield, William McKinley, and John F. Kennedy. All lay in state in the Rotunda of the Capitol while a grieving Nation paid them tribute.

There are no known pictures of Lincoln's services in the Capitol, but there are photographs showing all of the East Front columns circled with black bands and tied with large black bows to indicate that the Capitol was in mourning. After the death of Garfield on September 19th, 1881, *The Evening Critic,* a Washington paper, proclaimed in black-edged columns: "God Reigns. Clouds and Darkness May Surround Us, But the Government at Washington Will Live."

No black drapery appeared on public buildings in 1901 at the time of the assassination of William McKinley. A law had been passed prohibiting such decorations because of the increasing frequency of their use to mark the deaths of minor government officials. The decorations in the Rotunda planned for McKinley's lying-in-state would have been strikingly different had they been carried out. According to one newspaper report, a canopy circled with a cluster of electric lights had been built over the catafalque "so that the features of the dead president could be clearly seen" during the evening. However, a change in plans caused the viewing to close at dusk, so the electrified canopy was removed and the catafalque appeared "as it had been used by Lincoln and Garfield."

There is no law, written rule or regulation governing who may lie in state in the Rotunda. Use of the Rotunda is controlled, generally, by concurrent action of the Senate and House. However, the Rotunda has been used without full concurrence of both Houses, especially during adjournment or recess. The wishes of the family of a great individual are also respected by Congress.

There is no more appropriate place than the Rotunda of the Capitol to give honor to great servants of the people. In addition to the four Presidents who were killed while in office, there have been other Presidents and ex-Presidents accorded this same honor: Warren G. Harding in 1921, William Howard Taft in 1930, Herbert Hoover in 1964, Dwight D. Eisenhower in 1969, and Lyndon Baines Johnson in 1973. All have lain on the historic catafalque that was made for Abraham Lincoln. In all, twenty-four persons, including Senators, Representatives, and the Unknown Soldiers from World War I, World War II, and Korea, have been given this high tribute by a grateful people.

President Jimmy Carter consoles Mrs. Hubert H. Humphrey during funeral ceremonies in the Capitol Rotunda

Military honors. The horse drawn caisson and the riderless horse with the boots turned backward are two traditional symbols in a military funeral. The flag draped casket of former President Hoover is being removed from the caisson to be carried up the Senate steps and then to the Rotunda.

Those Who Have Lain in State in the Rotunda

Floral tribute. Indicative of the era when President Garfield was assassinated in 1881 were the elaborate decorations seen here around the casket in the Rotunda. This particular floral arrangement is referred to as the "Gate of Heaven" and parts of it have been preserved by the Smithsonian Institution.

Henry Clay: Lay in state in Rotunda July 1, 1852, following funeral service in Old Senate Chamber. Member of U.S. Senate from Kentucky four terms not consecutive from 1806 to 1852; Secretary of State 1825–1829; Member of House of Representatives three terms not consecutive from 1811 to 1825. During his terms in House, he also served as Speaker, 1811–1814, 1815–1820, 1823–1825. Died June 29, 1852, in Washington, D.C.

Abraham Lincoln: Lay in state in Rotunda April 19–21, 1865. President of United States March 4, 1861, until his death. Member of House of Representatives from Illinois March 4, 1847 to March 3, 1849. Shot by assassin April 14, 1865 in Washington, D.C. and died there April 15, 1865.

Thaddeus Stevens: Lay in state in Rotunda Aug. 13–14, 1868, prior to funeral service in Rotunda. Member of

Lying in state—
John Fitzgerald Kennedy

House of Representatives from Pennsylvania March 4, 1849, to March 3, 1853, and again from March 4, 1859, until his death. Died Aug. 11, 1868, in Washington, D.C.

Charles Sumner: Lay in state in Rotunda March 13, 1874 prior to funeral service in Senate Chamber. Member of U.S. Senate from Massachusetts April 24, 1851, until his death. Died March 11, 1874, in Washington, D.C.

Henry Wilson: Lay in state in Rotunda Nov. 25–26, 1875 prior to funeral service in Senate Chamber. Vice President of United States March 4, 1873, until his death. Member of U.S. Senate from Massachussets Jan. 31, 1855, to March 3, 1873, when he resigned to become Vice President. Died Nov. 22, 1875, in Vice President's room in Capitol, Washington, D.C.

James Abram Garfield: Lay in state in Rotunda Sept. 21–23, 1881, prior to funeral service in Rotunda. President of United States March 4, 1881, until his death. Member of House of Representatives from Ohio March 4, 1863, to Nov. 8, 1880, when he resigned, having been elected President. Shot by assassin July 2, 1881, in Washington, D.C. and died Sept. 19, 1881, in Elberon, New Jersey.

John Alexander Logan: Lay in state in Rotunda Dec. 30–31, 1886, prior to funeral service in Senate Chamber. Member of House of Representatives from Illinois March 4, 1859, to April 2, 1862, when he resigned to enter the Union Army, and again from March 4, 1867, until resignation on March 3, 1871, when elected Senator. Member of U.S. Senate March 4, 1871, to March 3, 1877. Died Dec. 26, 1886, in Washington, D.C.

William McKinley, Jr.: Lay in state in Rotunda Sept. 17, 1901, following funeral in Rotunda. President of United States March 4, 1897, until his death. Member of House of Representatives from Ohio March 4, 1877, to May 27, 1884, and again from March 4, 1885, to March 3, 1891. Shot by assassin Sept. 6, 1901, in Buffalo, New York, and died there Sept. 14, 1901.

Major Pierre Charles L'Enfant: (re-interment) Lay in state in Rotunda April 28, 1909, prior to memorial service in Rotunda. Planner of city of Washington, D.C. Died June 4, 1825, and was buried on Digges farm, Prince George's County, Maryland. Remains were brought to Capitol April 28,

1909. Remains were re-interred in Arlington National Cemetery.

Admiral George Dewey: Lay in state in Rotunda Jan. 20, 1917, during funeral service in Rotunda. Admiral of the Navy and hero of Manila Bay in Spanish American War. Died Jan. 16, 1917, in Washington, D.C.

Unknown Soldier of World War I: Lay in state in Rotunda Nov. 9–11, 1921. Chosen to honor and perpetuate the memory of the heroes who gave their lives in World War I. The body is that of an unknown American who served as a member of the American Expeditionary Forces in Europe and lost his life during World War I.

Warren Gamaliel Harding: Lay in state in Rotunda Aug. 8, 1923, following funeral service in Rotunda. President of United States March 4, 1921, until his death. Member of U.S. Senate from Ohio March 4, 1915 to Jan. 13, 1921, when he resigned, having been elected President. Died Aug. 2, 1923, in San Francisco, California.

Mrs. John F. Kennedy entering the Capitol Rotunda with the late Senator Robert Kennedy and Senator Edward Kennedy of Massachusetts for memorial services.

Endless lines. The term of President John F. Kennedy was limited to 1,000 days because of an assassin's bullet. Here is a scene typical of the crowds that streamed through the Rotunda for hours to pay homage to the fallen leader.

William Howard Taft: Lay in state in Rotunda March 11, 1930. President of United States March 4, 1909, to March 4, 1913. Chief Justice of U.S. Supreme Court June 30, 1921 (commission), July 11, 1921 (oath of office) to Feb. 3, 1930. Only man who served both as President and Chief Justice. Died March 8, 1930, in Washington, D.C.

General John Joseph Pershing: Lay in state in Rotunda July 18–19, 1948. General of the Armies of United States. Was graduated from U.S. Military Academy at West Point in 1886 and devoted his entire life to military service. Chief of Staff of the Army 1921–1924; Commander of American Expeditionary Forces, World War I; distinguished service during Philippine insurrection; and took part in Spanish American War. Died July 15, 1948, in Washington, D.C.

Robert Alphonso Taft: Lay in state in Rotunda Aug. 2–3, 1953, prior to memorial service in Rotunda. Member of U.S. Senate from Ohio Jan. 3, 1939, until his death. Died July 31, 1953, in New York City.

Unknown Soldiers of World War II and the Korean War: Lay in state in Rotunda May 28–30, 1958. Chosen to honor and perpetuate the memory of the heroes who gave their lives while serving overseas in the armed forces of the U.S. during World War II and the Korean War, and whose identities are unknown.

John Fitzgerald Kennedy: Lay in state in Rotunda Nov. 24–25, 1963, following memorial service in Rotunda. President of United States Jan. 20, 1961, until his death. Member of House of Representatives from Massachusetts Jan. 3, 1947, to Jan. 3, 1953. Member of U.S. Senate Jan. 3, 1953 to Dec. 22, 1960, when he resigned, having been elected President. Shot by assassin Nov. 22, 1963, in Dallas, Texas and died there.

General Douglas MacArthur: Lay in state in Rotunda April 8–9, 1964. Appointed General of the Army Dec. 18, 1944; Superintendent of U.S. Military Academy at West Point 1919–1922; appointed Chief of Staff of the Army Nov. 21, 1930. From July 26, 1941, through April 11, 1951, he served in Pacific and Far East in various allied commands. Died April 5, 1964, in Washington, D.C.

Herbert Clark Hoover: Lay in state in Rotunda Oct. 23–25, 1964. President of United States March 4, 1929, to March 3, 1933. Secretary of Commerce in cabinets of both Presidents Harding and Coolidge. Food Administrator under President Wilson. Chairman of Commission of Organization of Executive Branch of Government in 1947–1949 and 1953–1955. Died Oct. 20, 1964 in New York City.

Dwight David Eisenhower: Lay in state in Rotunda March 30–31, 1969. President of United States Jan. 20, 1953, to Jan. 20, 1961. Was graduated from U.S. Military Academy at West Point in 1915; promoted to General of the Army, 1944; named president of Columbia University 1948. Died March 28, 1969, in Washington, D.C.

Everett McKinley Dirksen: Lay in state in Rotunda Sept. 9–10, 1969, following memorial service in Rotunda. Member of U.S. Senate from Illinois Jan. 3, 1951, until his death. Member of House of Representatives March 4, 1933, to Jan. 3, 1949. Died Sept. 7, 1969, in Washington, D.C.

J. Edgar Hoover: Lay in state in Rotunda May 3–4, 1972, following memorial service in Rotunda. First Director of the Federal Bureau of Investigation, 1924 until his death. Died May 2, 1972, in Washington, D.C.

Lying in state—
Dwight David Eisenhower

Lyndon Baines Johnson: Lay in state in Rotunda January 24–25, 1973, following memorial service in Rotunda. President of United States Nov. 22, 1963, to Jan. 20, 1969. Member of House of Representatives from Texas April 10, 1937, to Jan. 3, 1949. Member of U.S. Senate Jan. 3, 1949, to Jan. 3, 1961, when he resigned, having been elected Vice President. Vice President Jan. 20, 1961, to Nov. 22, 1963. Died Jan. 22, 1973, at his ranch near Johnson City, Texas.

Hubert Horatio Humphrey: Lay in state in Rotunda January 14–15, 1978. Member of U.S. Senate from Nov. 3, 1970 until his death. Member U.S. Senate Jan. 3, 1949 to Dec. 29, 1964 when he resigned to become Vice President, Jan. 20, 1965 to Jan. 20, 1969. Died at his home in Waverly, Minnesota.

The services for the Honorable Hubert H. Humphrey were typical of the stirring simplicity of funerals in the Rotunda. The precision of the military honor guard, the lines of people, and the now ever present TV camera can be considered a pattern for funerals in the Capitol Rotunda.

Lying in state—
Lyndon Baines Johnson

Picture Credits

The editors of this publication are extremely grateful to the many persons and organizations who supplied the photographs. Though we would like to identify each photograph individually, there are so many sources involved that this is next to impossible. The following list shows the sources from which the pictures were gathered:

John Ahlers
Architect of the Capitol
Armed Service Bands
Broadcasting Magazine
Harry Burnett, Jr.
William McWhorter Cochrane
Corcoran Gallery of Art
Congressional Budget Office
Congressional Research Service
General Accounting Office
Government Printing Office
John O. Hamilton
Keith Jewell
Kiplinger Collection
Sal LaCapria
Library of Congress
Fred J. Maroon
Cynthia Watkins Meadow
Fred Mosedale
Alfonso A. Muto
National Archives
National Geographic Society
National Symphony
Office of Technology Assessment
Alan E. Porter
Roloc
Senate Curator of Arts and Antiquities
Senate Historian
Smithsonian Institution
United States Capitol Historical Society
Office of the Vice President
White House Photography Office

FOR SALE BY THE SUPERINTENDENT OF DOCUMENTS,
U.S. GOVERNMENT PRINTING OFFICE, WASHINGTON, D.C. 20402

STOCK NUMBER 052-071-00549-8

☆U.S. GOVERNMENT PRINTING OFFICE : 1979 O—98-588